Joe Sacco

PALESTINE

FANTAGRAPHICS BOOKS

DEDICATED TO KENJI, ERLIS, JAMILEH, JAD, JEMAL, AND SHAFEEK

Fantagraphics Books
7563 Lake City Way NE
Seattle, WA 98115

Cover colorist: Keeli McCarthy
Reprint cover design: Tony Ong
Editorial co-ordination: Kim Thompson
Associate Publisher: Eric Reynolds
Publisher: Gary Groth and Kim Thompson

Seventeenth printing: April 2017

ISBN: 978-1-56097-432-1
Library of Congress Control Number: 2015947334

Printed in Singapore

HOMAGE TO JOE SACCO

by Edward Said

omic books are a universal phenomenon associated with adolescence. They seem to exist in all languages and cultures, from East to West. In subject matter they go the whole range from inspired and fantastic to sentimental and silly; all of them, however, are easy to read, to pass around, store, and throw away. Many comics are like *Asterix* and *Tintin*, a continuing serial adventure for the young people who read them faithfully month after month; over time, like the two I mentioned, they seem to acquire a life of their own, with recurring characters, plot situations, and phrases that turn their readers—whether in Egypt, India or Canada—into a sort of club in which every member knows and can refer to a whole set of common assumptions and names. Most adults, I think, tend to connect comics with what is frivolous or ephemeral, and there is an assumption that as one grows older they are put aside for more serious pursuits, except very occasionally (as is the case with Art Spiegelman's *Maus*) when a forbiddingly grim subject is treated by a serious comic-book artist. But, as we shall soon see, these are very rare occasions indeed, since what is first of all required is a first-rate talent.

I don't remember when exactly I read my first comic book, but I do remember exactly how liberated and subversive I felt as a result. Everything about the enticing book of colored pictures, but specially its untidy, sprawling format, the colorful, riotous extravagance of its pictures, the unrestrained passage between what the characters thought and said, the exotic creatures and adventures reported and depicted: all this made up for a hugely wonderful thrill, entirely unlike anything I had hitherto known or experienced.

My incongruously Arab Protestant family and education in the colonial post World War II Middle East were very bookish and academically very demanding. An unremitting sobriety governed all things. These were certainly not the days either of television, or of numerous easily available entertainments. Radio was our link to the outside world, and because Hollywood films were considered both inevitable and somehow morally risky, we were kept to a regimen of one per week, each carefully vetted by my parents, certified by some unrevealed (to us) standard of judgment as acceptable and therefore not *bad* for children.

Not quite thirteen, I entered high school just after the fall of Palestine in 1948. Like all the mem-bers of my family, male and female, I was enrolled in British schools, which seemed to be modeled after their storybook equivalents in *Tom Brown's Schooldays* and the various accounts of Eton, Harrow, and Rugby that I had gleaned from my omnivorous reading of almost exclusively English books. In that late imperial setting of a highly conflicted world of mostly Arab and Levantine children, British teachers, in largely Muslim Arab countries themselves undergoing turbulent change, where the curriculum was based on the Oxford and Cambridge School Certificate (as the standardized English high school diploma was called in those days), the sudden intrusion of American comic books — which were instantly banned by parents and school authorities — burst like a small typhoon. In a matter of hours I was illicitly awash in a flood of Superman, Tarzan, Captain Marvel, and Wonder Woman adventures that boggled and certainly diverted my mind from the stricter and grayer things I should have been addressing.

Trying to reason why the ban against this pleasurable new world was so strict and seemed so rigidly enforced at home got me absolutely nowhere with my adamant parents except for the explanation that comics interfered with one's schoolwork. I have spent years trying to reconstruct the logic of the ban and have concluded over time that the prohibition very accurately grasped (certainly more than I did at the time) what it is that comics did so well and so uniquely. There were first of all such things as slang and violence, which ruffled the pretended calm of the learning process. Second, and perhaps more important though never stated, there was the release provided to my sexually repressed young life by outrageous characters (some of them like Sheena of the Jungle, dressed far too skimpily and sexily) who did and said things that could not be admitted either for reasons of probability and logic or, perhaps more crucially, because they violated conventional norms — norms of behavior, thought, accepted social forms. Comics played havoc with the logic of a+b+c+d and they certainly encouraged one not to think in terms of what the teacher expected or what a subject like history demanded. I vividly remember the elation I felt as I surreptitiously smuggled a copy of *Captain Marvel* in my briefcase and read it furtively on the bus or under the covers or in the back of the class. Besides, comics provided one with a directness of approach (the attractively and literally overstated combination of pictures and words) that seemed unassailably true on the one hand, and marvelously close, impinging, familiar on the other. In ways that I still find fascinating to decode, comics in their relentless foregrounding (far more, say, than film cartoons or funnies, neither of which mattered much to me) seemed to say what couldn't otherwise be said—perhaps what wasn't permitted to be said or imagined—defying the ordinary processes of thought, which are policed, shaped, and re-shaped by all sorts of pedagogical as well as ideological pressures. I knew nothing of this then, but I felt that comics freed me to think and imagine and see differently.

Cut now to the final decade of the twentieth century. As an American of Palestinian origin, I have found myself necessarily involved in the battle for Palestinian self-determination and human rights. Sidelined by distance, illness, and exile, my role has been to defend this most difficult cause, to defend and attempt to portray its complicated and often-suppressed dimensions in writing and speaking in public, all the while trying to keep up with the unfolding of our history as a people in places like Amman, Beirut, and then finally, when I was able to return to Palestine in 1992 for the first time since my family and I left Jerusalem in 1947, on the actual West Bank and Gaza.

When I began this effort just after the June 1967 War, even the word "Palestine" was next to impossible to use in public discourse. I recall signs carried outside teach-ins and lectures on Palestine in that period blaring "there is no Palestine," and in 1969 Golda Meir made her famous statement saying that the Palestinians did not exist. Much of my work as a writer and lecturer was concerned with refuting the misrepresentations and dehumanizations of our history, trying at the same time to

by Edward Said

give the Palestinian narrative — so effectively blotted out by the media and legions of antagonistic polemicists — a presence and a human shape.

Without any warning or preparation, about ten years ago my young son brought home Joe Sacco's first comic book on Palestine. Cut off as I was from the world of active comic reading, trading and bartering, I had no idea at all that Sacco or his gripping work existed. I was plunged directly back into the world of the first great intifada (1987–92) and, with even greater effect, back into the animated, enlivening world of the comics I had read so long ago. The shock of recognition was therefore a double one, and the more I read compulsively in Sacco's *Palestine* comic-books—of which there are about ten, all of them now collected into one volume which I hope will make them widely available not only to American readers but all over the world—the more convinced I was that here was a political and aesthetic work of extraordinary originality, quite unlike any other in the long, often turgid and hopelessly twisted debates that had occupied Palestinians, Israelis, and their respective supporters.

As we also live in a media-saturated world in which a huge preponderance of the world's news images are controlled and diffused by a handful of men sitting in places like London and New York, a stream of comic-book images and words, assertively etched, at times grotesquely emphatic and distended to match the extreme situations they depict, provide a remarkable antidote. In Joe Sacco's world there are no smooth-talking announcers and presenters, no unctuous narrative of Israeli triumphs, democracy, achievements, no assumed and reconfirmed representations — all of them disconnected from any historical or social source, from any lived reality — of Palestinians as rock-throwing, rejectionist, and fundamentalist villains whose main purpose is to make life difficult for the peace-loving, persecuted Israelis. What we get instead is seen through the eyes and persona of a modest-looking, ubiquitous crew-cut young American man who appears to have wandered into an unfamiliar, inhospitable world of military occupation, arbitrary arrest, harrowing experiences of houses demolished and land expropriated, torture ("moderate physical pressure"), and sheer brute force generously, if cruelly, applied (e.g., an Israeli soldier refusing to let people through a roadblock on the West Bank because, he says, revealing an enormous, threatening set of teeth, of THIS, the M-16 rifle he brandishes) at whose mercy Palestinians live on a daily, indeed hourly basis.

There's no obvious spin, no easily discernible line of doctrine in Joe Sacco's often ironic encounters with Palestinians under occupation, no attempt to smooth out what is for the most part a meager, anxious existence of uncertainty, collective unhappiness, and deprivation, and, especially in the Gaza comics, a life of aimless wandering within the place's inhospitable confines, wandering and mostly waiting, waiting, waiting. With the exception of one or two novelists and poets, no one has ever rendered this terrible state of affairs better than Joe Sacco. Certainly his images are more graphic than anything you can either read or see on television. With his friend, the Japanese photographer Saburo (who seems to get lost at one point), Joe is a listening, watchful presence, sometimes skeptical, sometimes fed up, but mostly sympathetic and funny, as he notes that a cup of Palestinian tea is often drowned in sugar, or how perhaps involuntarily they congregate in order to exchange tales of woe and suffering, the way fishermen compare the size of their catch or hunters the stealth of their prey.

The cast of characters in the many episodes collected here is wondrously varied and, with the comic draughtsman's uncanny ability to catch the telling detail—a carefully sculpted mustache here, overly large teeth there, a drab suit here—Sacco manages to keep it all going with almost careless virtuosity. The unhurried pace and the absence of a goal in his wanderings emphasizes that he is neither a journalist in search of a story nor an expert trying to nail down the facts in order to produce a policy. Joe is there to be in Palestine, and only that — in effect to spend as much time as he can sharing, if not finally living the life that Palestinians are condemned to lead. Given the realities of power and his identification with the underdog, Sacco's Israelis are depicted with an unmistakable skepticism, if not always distrust. Mostly they are figures of unjust power and dubious authority. I am not referring only to obviously unattractive personages like the many soldiers and settlers who keep popping up to make life for Palestinians difficult and deliberately unbearable but, especially in one telling episode, even the so-called peaceniks whose support for Palestinian rights appears so hedged, so timid, and finally ineffective as to make them also objects of disappointed scorn.

Joe is there to find out why things are the way they are and why there seems to have been an impasse for so long. He is drawn to the place partly because (we learn from an exceptionally weird earlier comic, *War Junkie*) of his Maltese family background during World War II, partly because the postmodern world is so accessible to the young and curious American, partly because like Joseph Conrad's Marlow he is tugged at by the forgotten places and people of the world, those who don't make it on to our television screens, or if they do, who are regularly portrayed as marginal, unimportant, perhaps even negligible were it not for their nuisance value which, like the Palestinians, seems impossible to get rid of. Without losing the comics' unique capacity for delivering a kind of surreal world as animated and in its own way as arrestingly violent as a poet's vision of things, Joe Sacco can also unostentatiously transmit a great deal of information: the human context and historical events that have reduced Palestinians to their present sense of stagnating powerlessness, despite the peace process and despite the sticky gloss put on things by basically hypocritical leaders, policy-makers, and media pundits.

Nowhere does Sacco come closer to the existential lived reality of the average Palestinian than in his depiction of life in Gaza, the national Inferno. The vacancy of time, the drabness—not to say sordidness—of everyday life in the refugee camps, the network of relief workers, bereaved mothers, unemployed young men, teachers, police, hangers-on, the ubiquitous tea or coffee circle, the sense of confinement, permanent muddiness, and ugliness conveyed by the refugee camp which is so iconic to the whole Palestinian experience: these are rendered with almost terrifying accuracy and, para-doxically enough, gentleness at the same time. Joe the character is there sympathetically to understand and to try to experience not only why Gaza is so representative a place in its hopelessly overcrowded and yet rootless spaces of Palestinian dispossession, but also to affirm that it is there, and must somehow be accounted for in human terms, in the narrative sequences with which any reader can identify.

If you pay attention, therefore, you will note the scrupulous rendering of the generations, how children and adults make their choices and live their meager lives, how some speak and some remain silent, how they are dressed in the drab sweaters, miscellaneous jackets, and warm *hattas* of an improvised life—on the fringes of their homeland in which they have become that saddest and most powerless and contradictory of creatures, the unwelcome alien. You can see this all in a sense through Joe's own eyes as he moves and tarries among them, attentive, unaggressive, caring, ironic—and so his visual testimony becomes himself, himself so to speak in his own comics, in an act of the profoundest solidarity. Above all, his Gaza series animates and confirms what three other remarkable witnesses before him, all of them women, have written about (one of them Israeli, another one American-Jewish, a third one an American with no previous connection with the Middle East) so unforgettably: Amira Hass, the brave Israeli *Ha'aretz* correspondent who lived in and wrote about Gaza for four years, Sara Roy, who wrote the definitive study of how Gaza's economy was de-developed, and Gloria Emerson, prize-winning journalist and novelist who gave a year of her time to live among the people of Gaza.

But what finally makes Sacco so unusual a portrayer of life in the Occupied Palestinian Territories is that his true concern is finally history's victims. Recall that most of the comics we read almost routinely conclude with someone's victory, the triumph of good over evil, or the routing of the unjust by the just, or even the marriage of two young lovers. Superman's villains get thrown out and we hear of and see them no more. Tarzan foils the plans of evil white men and they are shipped out of Africa in disgrace. Sacco's *Palestine* is not at all like that. The people he lives among are history's losers, banished to the fringes where they seem so despondently to loiter, without much hope or organization, except for their sheer indomitability, their mostly unspoken will to go on, and their willingness to cling to their story, to retell it, and to resist designs to sweep them away altogether. Astutely, Sacco seems to distrust militancy, particularly of the collective sort that bursts out in slogans or verbal flag-waving. Neither does he try to provide *solutions* of the kind that have made such a mockery of the Oslo peace process. But his comics about Palestine furnish his readers with a long enough sojourn among a people whose suffering and unjust fate have been scanted for far too long and with too little humanitarian and political attention. Sacco's art has the power to detain us, to keep us from impatiently wandering off in order to follow a catch-phrase or a lamentably predictable narrative of triumph and fulfillment, and this is perhaps the greatest of his achievements.

AUTHOR'S FOREWORD
to the complete edition of *Palestine*

This book collects all nine issues of a comic-book series called *Palestine* under one cover for the first time. Previously, the series had been collected in two volumes. I wrote and drew *Palestine* after spending two months in the Occupied Territories almost ten years ago in the winter of 1991–92. Since that visit, a "peace process" was initiated, culminating in a number of agreements or near-agreements — some highly touted as "breakthrough" — and the installation of a Palestine Authority headed by Yasser Arafat in some areas from which the Israelis have withdrawn. While Nobel Peace Prizes have been awarded, no major outstanding issues — the return of or compensation for Palestinian refugees, the illegal Jewish settlements, the status of Jerusalem — have been resolved. (As far as the settlers go, they have continued to add to their number by the tens of thousands.) But even if you skip over those difficult points — and you can't — the "peace process" has not provided the Palestinian people living in territory conquered by Israel in 1967 with many tangible benefits. In fact, their land is still expropriated, their dwellings are still bulldozed, their olive groves are still uprooted. They still encounter an occupying army, as well as the settlers, who are often the armed adjuncts to the occupying army (or vice versa, it's hard to tell sometimes). Through closures and the lasting effect of long-term strangulation by Israel of the Palestinian economy, the lives of Palestinian workers and their families have been made even more wretched than they were when this work was first published. One must add the mismanagement and corruption of the Palestine Authority into the unfortunate mix.

This book is about the first intifada against the Israeli occupation, which was beginning to run out of steam at the time of my visit. As I write these words, a second intifada is taking place because, in short, Israeli occupation, and all the consequences of the domination of one people by another, has not ceased. The Palestinian and Israeli people will continue to kill each other in low-level conflict or with shattering violence — with suicide bombers or helicopter gunships and jet bombers — until this central fact, Israeli occupation, is addressed as an issue of international law and basic human rights.

Joe Sacco
July 2001

Chapter One

It was far into the a.m., we'd been drinking, and Claudia, who was half Iraqi, who'd studied Arabic in Damascus where she'd left her Palestinian Romeo whose first names with Yasser— Claudia may or may not have brother in the PLO was on first names said something of interest at that point...

You better believe I did:

AMERICANS WON'T CARE ABOUT THE PROBLEMS OF PALESTIN-IANS WHEN AMERICANS GET KILLED IN THESE TERRORIST ATTACKS. ONE AMERICAN DIES LIKE THAT, IT ECLIPSES ANY-THING PALESTINIANS HAVE TO SAY!

WELL... I DON'T KNOW SO MUCH ABOUT THESE THINGS...

I knew she did, but...

Conversation over!

A peck on the cheek and—

I went home alone

PALESTINIAN BOYFRIEND! HA! BITCH! TERRORIST GROUPIE!

Unfair? You bet, but I couldn't get the taste out of my mouth, terrorism is the bread Palestinians get buttered on, I'd swallowed that ever since the airliners went sky high in the desert, do you remember that, do you remember Munich and the blown up athletes, the bus and airport massacres?

J. SACCO 8·92

7

I do, my mind gurgles over with televised pools of blood.... I mean sure I had sympathy for a homeland lost, but what were the problems of Palestinians to me next to Klinghoffer, who ate Brand X corn flakes and probably borrowed my ladder...

He went over the side of the Achille Lauro and into my consciousness.

And if Palestinians have been sinking for decades, ex-pelled, bombed and kicked black and blue, even when it's made the evening news I never caught a name or recall a face, to say nothing about their corn flakes. But now my buddy on the West Bank wants to make some introductions, to set me up, he wants me to shake hands with his people's pain...

THIS WOMAN, SHE HAS EIGHT CHILDREN. HER HUSBAND VERY OLD, VERY SICK. THE GOVERNMENT GIVES HER NOTHING!

J. SACCO 8·92

8

RETURN

"Next year in Jerusalem"—all over the world that's the Jewish toast at Passover, and now here he is, a Jew in Zion, a land promised by God to his chosen people:

EVERY PLACE THAT THE SOLE OF YOUR FOOT WILL TREAD UPON I HAVE GIVEN TO YOU AS I PROMISED MOSES. FROM THE WILDERNESS AND THIS LEBANON AS FAR AS THE GREAT RIVER EUPHRATES, ALL THE LAND OF THE HITTITES TO, ETC....

JOSHUA 1:3

GOD

And in 1917—after two millennia of Jewish Diaspora—the British dusted off the promise of the Lord. Great Powers had Big Battleships back then, Broad Pen-strokes, too, and plenty of India Ink. Lord Balfour signed his declaration and the Zionists had a British commitment to a homeland in Palestine for the Jews.

A LAND WITHOUT A PEOPLE FOR A PEOPLE WITHOUT A LAND!

J. SACCO 9·92

But things weren't as cut and dry as _that_ Zionist slogan. Plenty of Arabs lived in Palestine; in 1917 Arabs outnumbered Jewish inhabitants ten-to-one. But you know mathematics, it doesn't always fit into the equation:

LORD BALFOUR AGAIN

ZIONISM, BE IT RIGHT OR WRONG, GOOD OR BAD, IS ROOTED IN AGE-LONG TRADITION, IN PRESENT NEEDS, IN FUTURE HOPES, OF FAR PROFOUNDER IMPORT THAN THE DESIRE AND PREJUDICES OF 700,000 ARABS WHO NOW INHABIT THAT ANCIENT LAND.

And, incidentally:

WE DO NOT PROPOSE EVEN TO GO THROUGH THE FORM OF CONSULTING THE WISHES OF THE PRESENT INHABITANTS OF THE COUNTRY.

Decision made! History follows on such heels and refugees after that... But if it's been downhill for Palestinians ever since, Israelis have soared to greater heights, who can deny it?

J. SACCO 9·92

13

Chapter Two

CARRY ON, DOCTOR

Okay, the 11-year-old from the last page... definitely a sweetie... my heart's still melted... But let's put the issue of cuteness aside (along with the Fourth Geneva Convention) ...it's not exactly like she was not guilty ...on a second visit, she 'fesses up...

I TRIED TO THROW A STONE, BUT THE SOLDIERS WERE FASTER...

...armed with M-16s, too, and Galil assault rifles...

But there's fewer clashes these days and less of the acute-response-to-impact stuff that grabbed world attention from late '87 to '88, the first year of the intifada, when 400 Palestinians were killed, 20,000 injured, when Israeli Defense Minister Yitzhak Rabin ordered the crushing of protests with "force, might, and beatings" and Prime Minister Yitzhak Shamir called for putting "the fear of death into the Arabs of the areas..."

TODAY WE HAVE ONLY FOUR BULLET INJURIES IN THE MEN'S SECTION.

At the worst of the violence, the nurse says, the hospital had 20 casualties at a time; gunshot cases from Jenin, Tulkarm, and as far away as Ramallah spilled over into the female ward, sometimes into the maternity section...

In those days when the "shebab" —the youth— heard ambulances they'd come quickly from school, from university, to give blood, a medical technician tells me...

Now the hospital's got a special refrigerator for plasma, she says... it keeps for a year... they're well stocked...

BUT AS IN ALL WARS FRESH BLOOD IS BEST.

J. SACCO 11-92

And what's that scar on her neck? Oh, a bullet in the throat she picked up at Bir Zeit University while protesting a killing at Bethlehem University... three major surgeries...

Anyway, she says, after clashes soldiers often follow ambulances in, they enter the emergency room to interrogate the wounded...

Soldiers do what they want, she says, they come into the operating theater without masks, they question visitors, they've shouted at people donating blood, they've beaten her director. Other staffers tell me of soldiers obstructing ambulances, of taking patients "right from the [operating] theater...."

IT'S AN ORDINARY CASE TO WORK UNDER TENSION.

The last incident? "Two weeks ago soldiers came in and did a quick search, not a very serious one, they checked the W.C.

"They ordered all employees into the courtyard, except those in the operating room ... All the other patients we left unattended ... No one was allowed in or out..."

J. SACCO 11·92

"We stood in the cold for half an hour. I was shaking with cold. They said all female employees could go back in, but we refused..."

"They checked our ID cards and took five male employees in a jeep. I told the soldiers not to beat them..."

"They released two of them later. A third one they brought back to the hospital because he was ill. They kept his ID card to make sure he would return to jail."

The others?

WE DON'T KNOW ABOUT THEM YET.

J. SACCO 11-92

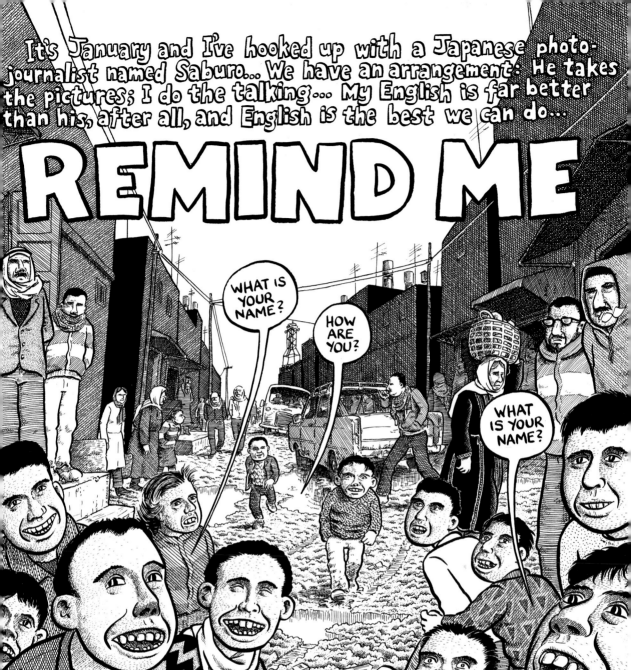

It's January and I've hooked up with a Japanese photo-journalist named Saburo... We have an arrangement: He takes the pictures; I do the talking... My English is far better than his, after all, and English is the best we can do...

REMIND ME

WHAT IS YOUR NAME?

HOW ARE YOU?

WHAT IS YOUR NAME?

Not that English always gets you far, but the kids like the practice, and it's a good idea to get the kids on your side. I smile a lot, tell them my name is Joe, that I am fine, and that usually does the trick, though not always. Two or three times, in other places, kids have chased me off, calling out to each other that I'm a Jew, or picked up stones and fingered them till I've smiled and beamed my

way into their little hearts. Kids can be exhausting...

Adults, too. Not that _they_ run after you, giggling and tugging at your sleeve. In a place like this they hang back, staring, sizing up the kind of trouble you might mean. More smiles and greetings in order here. "Salaam Aleekum!" Keep that smile going. "Salaam Aleekum!" _Now_ they're smiling back. Someone hands us a bag of tangerines.

This is Balata, the biggest refugee camp in the West Bank, practically across the road from Nablus. Some Palestinians living here were among the three-quarters of a million who fled or were forced out of what is now Israel in 1948...

Do we need to talk about 1948? It's hardly a secret how the Zionists used rumors, threats, and massacres to expel the Arabs and create new demographics that guaranteed the Jewish nature of Israel.

Of course, it's more comfortable to think of refugees as some regrettable consequence of war, but getting rid of the Palestinians has been an idea kicking around since Theodor Herzl formulated modern Zionism in the late 1800s. "We shall have to spirit the penniless population [sic] across the border," he wrote, "by procuring employment for it in the transit countries, while denying it employment in our own country."

After all, some Zionists reasoned, Palestinians were less attached to their ancestral homeland than the Jews who hadn't lived there for centuries. According to Israel's first prime minister, David Ben-Gurion, a Palestinian "is equally at ease whether in Jordan, Lebanon or a variety of places." With war imminent, Ben-Gurion had no illusions about "spiriting" or inducing the Palestinians away. "In each attack," he wrote, "a decisive blow should be struck, resulting in the destruction of homes and the expulsion of the population." When that was basically accomplished he told an advisor, "Palestinian Arabs have only one role left — to flee."

DAVID BEN-GURION

J. SACCO 12-92

But if 1948 is no secret, it's all but a non-issue, dismissed entirely by Prime Minister Golda Meir: "It was not as though there was a Palestinian people considering itself as a Palestinian people and we came and threw them out and took their country away from them. They did not exist."

GOLDA MEIR

But they **did** exist, and they **do**, and here they are... and their children, and their children's children... and **still** they are refugees... stale ones, maybe, in the nightly news scheme of things, but, nonetheless, refugees... which I suppose means they're waiting to go back...

But back to what? Close to 400 Palestinian villages were razed by the Israelis during and after the '48 war... fleeing Palestinians were declared "absentees" ...their homes and lands declared "abandoned" or "uncultivated" and expropriated for settlement by Jews.

You say refugee camp and I picture tents, people lying on cots... but somewhere along the line Balata's residents figured they'd be here for the long haul, and the camp took on a sort of shabby

permanence... People live here, they watch T.V., they shop, they raise families... On first glance, sloshing down a main road, what sets Balata apart is the mud. The snows have melted and the road is mud. Everywhere, mud.

We came here to meet Saburo's friend, but he's gone to a wedding somewhere and won't be back today. Now what? I'm freezing, and I wonder how long we're going to walk around in the cold.

Fortunately someone remembers Saburo from last time he was here and invites us into his shop for tea... ah, tea... holding a cup of tea, that's the ticket for right now... I'm lost in my tea while Saburo arranges a place to spend the night.

Meanwhile, word must be out 'cause small groups of the shebab are coming and going, giving us the once over. Most of them hang out for a few minutes and leave. Foreigners? Journalists? Big deal! We're not the first and won't be the last to drop by looking under their skirts for stories...

One of them, though, maybe he's 16 or 18, takes a shining to me. It must be all my smiling. His English is piss-poor, but that doesn't stop a guy like this, pantomime's not beneath him. He makes it clear he's done some rough-and-tumble with the IDF, the Israeli Defense Forces. He takes out his ID card to prove it. Every Palestinian over 16 in the Occupied Territories has to carry one, and his is green, which means he's done a recent stint in prison. He orders over a friend who sheepishly produces an orange ID, the regular card color for West Bank residents.

"Green card: Intifada!" says my new pal, waving his card... "Orange card: No intifada," he says, holding up his friend's...

Orange Card retreats with a red face while Green Card beams proudly. I beam back, out of sympathy, really, 'cause I've got a bad feeling about a dude without discretion like this... He's destined for a casualty appendix, I'm thinking; he's probably got an appointment with a serious bullet.

Saburo's made arrangements for the night. We'll be staying with someone named Jabril, who speaks pretty good English. Jabril takes us home, sits us down in the front room, makes us comfy. There's full mobilization in the kitchen and he and his brothers bring out one plate after another. It's a regular feast! I tell you, I eat like a king in refugee camps, they pull out all the stops, I blow kisses in the direction of the invisible womenfolk. And now we're stuffed, and Jabril sets up the kerosene heater against our toes, he wants us crispy.

"Coffee?" he asks.

Christ, they love us in Palestine!

Meanwhile, the room's filling with neighbors. They've heard about us and they don't mind answering some questions. I reach for my pad. They've been laughing

43

and talking amongst themselves, but now they're quiet, even the children they've brought along.

I ask where they work. "Israel! Israel!" say most. There's jobs in Israel, they say, not in the West Bank. They get up early for their jobs. It's an hour there, an hour back, and they have to be out of the country by 6 p.m. Only Jabril has a local job, in Nablus. The others are part of Israel's convenient low-wage labor pool. Israel calls the economic shots and makes rules to suit itself, as when Defense Minister Rabin said in 1985: "No permits will be given for expanding agriculture or industry [in the Territories] which may compete with the State of Israel."

Mahmoud says he hasn't worked for two years. He has a green ID card, which means he can't cross into Israel for work. Green card? He was in prison? The soldiers came to his door one day, he says, he asked why and they smashed him in the head! In front of his wife and children! The soldiers wanted to know who was throwing stones. Mahmoud told them it wasn't him, but they took him anyway. He shrugs. "If they don't take me, they'll take you."

Now they're all blurting stories about soldiers and prisons. Firas says soldiers shot him two years ago and his leg's still not right. Ahmed says soldiers raided his home at midnight, they busted down the door, they came through the roof, they destroyed furniture, they caught him. He was 16. Three years in prison. "For what?" I ask. "For throwing a Molotov cocktail," he says. "And I didn't even see where it landed." The whole crowd

44

busts up. They think that's pretty funny.

But the Israelis take Molotovs seriously, often demolishing the homes of Molotov throwers. I ask about demolished homes in Balata. They talk it over, pointing different directions, counting on their fingers, naming names.

"Six houses destroyed by dynamite," Abu Akram announces finally. "One of them belonged to my friend, a butcher, he was a rich man. Eleven other people lived in his house. They had one hour to move." The butcher, it seems, was a collaborator who was discovered and allowed to redeem himself by killing two other collaborators, who were considered dangerous. He killed them; the Israelis put him in prison for life, blew up his home. They say five collaborators have been killed in Balata.

I ask about life in the camp. "No cinema, no garden," says Jabril. "If the soldier sees me he asks, 'Where are you going?' If I want to play football in the schoolyard, the soldier comes. So my friends visit my home. We drink tea. We drink coffee. We speak. This is my life."

Jabril says Balata has a reputation with the soldiers. The first West Bank clashes of the intifada occurred here. Jabril says he's been knocked down in Nablus by soldiers who've discovered he's from Balata.

"When I go to Nablus," says Abu Akram, "I go with a hurry and come back. If a soldier stops me, he puts me up against a wall, takes my card, he asks the computer, he asks why I was in prison. If the soldier is very bad, he takes me in a store and beats me. It is best to stay in Balata camp."

We go on the roof. It's freezing up there, but the lights from a nearby

45

Jewish settlement are pretty. It's almost 8 o'clock and the party splits up. No one wants to be caught by soldiers after curfew.

Jabril is exhausted from translating, but the night is still young and he feels an obligation, I suppose, to entertain us. He sets up a video player and we watch 'The Delta Force,' starring Chuck Norris and Lee Marvin. The film is sort of based on a hijacking in the mid-'80s where a U.S. soldier was murdered and several Americans held hostage in Beirut. Eventually the hostages were released. In the movie, however, the Delta Force gets to rescue the hostages à la Entebbe and wipe out scores of Palestinian terrorists to boot. And while the Americans stand together and defiant against their tormentors, the snivelling Palestinians betray their cause en masse when presented with personal

CHUCK NORRIS

harm. Jabril and his brothers mostly watch impassively, shaking their heads from time to time as Palestinians run screaming from battle or are blown

to bits by Norris from his rocket-firing motorcycle.

After the video, they prepare mats for us on the floor. Jabril has the couch. He plays a cassette softly to fall asleep to. I recognize the voice— Oum Koulsoum, the Egyptian singer who died years ago. My friend Taha in Cairo told me her funeral was bigger than Sadat's. She wasn't much to look at, sort

OUM KOULSOUM

of like Roy Orbison on a bad day, but what a voice! What a performance! It's obviously a love song... the audience is gasping, I'm gasping, too; I'm like the audience, overwhelmed. The song goes on and on. Jabril flips the cassette. The song is still going.

"What song is this?" I ask. "'Fakarouni,'" Jabril answers; "Remind Me."

Jabril is playing the song for his fiancée in Jordan. She's Palestinian, too, also a refugee... The Israelis won't let her visit because she has no immediate family members left in Palestine to apply for her visa... And Jabril can't go to her. The Israelis won't let him out of the country

any more. They accused him of traveling on to Syria on his last visit to Jordan. They accused him of training for terrorist missions with George Habash's Popular Front for the Liberation of Palestine. They accused him of training for terrorist missions in Japan. Japan?... They came for him at night and took him to Nablus prison and interrogated him for two months. They beat him, they kept him from sleeping, they— But we can talk about that some other time, he says. He has to get up early for work.

When Saburo and I wake up, Jabril is already gone... As usual, I'm shivering. The water's too cold to wash with.

This morning we want to check out one of Balata's preparatory schools administered by the United Nations Relief and Works Agency... UNRWA... which tends to some basic needs of Palestinian refugees. We walk to the school but they won't let us in, not without higher authorization. They put me on the phone with the UNRWA area office in Nablus. "You understand we need to take certain security precautions," explains the guy on the other end. "You've seen the situation there." He can give us authorization, if we come in to Nablus. We take the short taxi ride to town and the UNRWA official waves us into his office and dashes off a handwritten pass. We're all set, we're on the UNRWA guest list.

On the way to catch a taxi back to Balata, Saburo gets

a wild hair up his ass and decides he's going to get photos of Nablus prison. Nablus prison? With all it's barbed wire and watch-towers and guards and "NO PHOTOGRAPHY" signs posted clearly? He gives me all the film he's taken in case soldiers pick him up. And off he goes.

I get to the taxi stand where I see Abu Akram from last night's discussion. He comes over, we shake hands, and then we both notice a soldier in a red beret making his way in our direction. Suddenly, Abu Akram's gone! He and some pals are running through the traffic, and Red Beret's running after them... the Palestinians hop aboard a taxi that's already in motion just as Red Beret is upon them... and Red Beret suddenly gives up his pursuit... maybe it wasn't a pursuit, maybe everyone was out for a run... I don't know... I'm already in a taxi clutching Saburo's film bag, feeling dizzy and like some-how I'm to blame.

Back in Balata, I'm sitting in the headmaster's office and he still won't let me into the school. Like an idiot, I've left my signed permission with an UNRWA dude at an office down the road. Three schoolboys have gone to retrieve it, but they haven't returned, and school's almost out. Come back tomorrow, says the headmaster. Be patient, says the teacher doing the translating. He says Israelis have come into the camp posing as journalists before... they've "interviewed" students

and found out who the activists are... then the soldiers have come to make arrests...

Saburo shows up about the time the bell ends the school day. We step outside and are surround-ed by kids asking our names and religions, which we answer several times... The teacher comes out of the office and shoos them away... He's joined by a colleague and they agree to show us around, per-

mission or not.

They take us to a class-room. No electricity, no heat, they say, it's been like this for 40 years. "They thought the school was temporary when they built it," says one. "They thought they'd go back to their homes [in Israel] in a year or two." UNRWA is promising electricity, he says, but the students had to strike for it. They show us where the rain drips into the classroom. They

47

They ordered him to take down a picture of Arafat from a wall. Yes, but why did they beat him? "For speaking to them in English and not in Hebrew," he says.

Saburo and I make a quick visit to the local UNRWA clinic. They don't ask for authorization here. A nurse gives us a tour of the antenatal department—50 camp births a month, she says; the laboratory; the rehabilitation unit; and (with some pride) the new X-ray room.

Now the doctor will see us. The nurse jumps us past the long line waiting at his door. The doctor greets us into his office and shoos out a couple of female patients.

Just two doctors serve the clinic, he says, one of them a relief doctor. "The main problem," he says, "is overload." The clinic gets up to 300 patients a day. (Last night, at the roundtable discussion, the men joked about the rushed diagnoses at the clinic. "Go to the window! Go to the window!" they sang, mimicking the staff sending them away with hurried prescriptions.)

The doctor says he sees a lot of respiratory illnesses from bad ventilation and overcrowding, "from problems related to political and social conditions."

Meanwhile, there's knocking on the door! We've been too long! The women who've been kicked out want back in! Whose clinic is it, anyway?

Outside we find Green Card —Mr. Intifada from yesterday—and a friend. They've

show us the outdoor toilets whose walls have crumbled.

The headmaster appears, he has angry words for the teachers. The three of them step aside, arguing, apparently, on the advisability of talking to "journalists." The teachers are raising their voices. The headmaster walks off sullenly. The teachers rejoin us. "Never mind," one of them says. "We told him we take full responsibility."

They tell us their curriculum corresponds to Jordan's. The Israelis allow English and math books in from Jordan, they say, but no history or geography text, for example, that mentions Palestine. Not that it matters, says one teacher. "Since the intifada it is not necessary to teach such children that this is not Israel."

They say soldiers pass by ...soldiers chase people through the school...they shoot... it doesn't make for a good school environment for the 500 boys. What about for teachers? On a recent morning, says one of them, on his way to school, soldiers beat him.

come to fetch us. For what? Their English isn't good enough to explain. We follow them. I've become familiar with Balata's main roads, but they lead us into the maze of side streets, into the back alleys, where there's hardly a couple of shoulder-widths between houses and little boys are playing marbles... We're twisting and turning... hopping over open drainage canals... going left, going right, going in circles, I can't tell. Period-ically Green Card motions for us to stop, peers around a corner, motions for us to follow. "Police danger," he informs us. He stops us again. They frisk us. They go through our belongings. Green Card turns the pages of my passport, he studies leftover bank receipts from

Cairo, my air ticket, my camera... He's flipping through my journals... He's serious, grim even... Of course, I could have reams of notes about a hot-tubbing experience with Ariel Sharon and Green Card wouldn't have a clue ... In any case, they decide we're kosher... more twists and turns... we're back on a muddy main street ... whew...

Now we're in a house, the tea is coming... Jabril is there, and a few faces from the night before... but there's someone new... you'd figure after all the precautions Green Card took we'd be meeting Arafat himself or at least a Black Panthers guerrilla, but this new fellow looks pretty ordinary... and his spiel isn't anything I haven't

heard before... He's vague about who he is, though, and I don't press him for a resume.

He says the uprising is the result of years of suffering, that the intifada started spontaneously but is now directed by the PLO. He says the intifada focused world attention on the Palestinians and now there's a chance for a political solution...

That's the tip-off. This guy's with Fateh, Arafat's faction of the PLO... I've made a game of guessing what PLO faction a Pales-tinian supports by his opinion of the "peace process"... Popular Front supporters, for example, oppose the talks 'cause of stiff Israeli preconditions on the Palestinian negot-iating team.

He says Balata is mainly

J.SACCO 12-92

49

with Fateh. Fateh supports the negotiations, so he supports the negotiations ...but he's a skeptic. "The majority of Israelis don't want land-for-peace," he says. "They want to make agreements with other Arab nations, but not with Palestinians." What does he see ahead? "More settlements, more soldiers, more [Jewish] immigration." And if the negotiations fail, then what? "What do you expect?" he says. "The intifada will continue."

The discussion's over. The women are sending in food. We're dipping pita bread into all kinds of stuff. We're off politics now. We're laughing. Here comes the coffee...

They're asking Saburo about Japan, and I turn his rough English into English they can understand. It comes out that Saburo is something of a spiritualist, he reads lifelines... Green Card pulls his chair up and sticks out his palm. After a little analysis, Saburo has complimentary words about Green Card's emotions and intelligence... Then Saburo looks hard at the palm and announces that something will happen to Green Card soon. "Back in jail," says Jabril and they all laugh. "No," insists Saburo, "things will get better."

They warn us about the upcoming strikes... Hamas, the Islamic fundamentalist group, has called a general strike for tomorrow; the Unified National Leader-

ship has called one for the day after; and both groups have called for a strike the day after that ... That's going to mess up the taxi situation. We decide to split rather than get stranded in Balata.

We take a taxi to Nablus ...the Nablus streets are all but empty; maybe there's a curfew coming up ...At the taxi stand we find a Jerusalem-bound stretch Mercedes and wait inside with a couple and their boy. The driver won't leave till he gets one or two more passengers, but we'll have to leave soon if we want to get through Ramallah before Ramallah's five o'clock curfew...

A jeep pulls up across the street. Soldiers jump out and head into a narrow Old City passageway.

There's a gunshot...Another jeep pulls up. More soldiers. A soldier with a radio drops his phone and it swings wildly out of reach below his knees. He can't seem to get at it. He's having trouble. The boy in the taxi is laughing, calling the soldier "mignoon"—crazy. His father says to roll up the windows in case there's gas... Another jeep shows up. More soldiers are piling out and ducking into the passageway.

And finally we're leaving Nablus... past the prison ...We're leaving Balata behind ...Balata is receding... I'm looking forward to the long, winding hilly stretch ahead... Jerusalem is one hour away... Jerusalem is one hour away... meanwhile, I'll enjoy the scenery.

Chapter Three

The woman of the house lets us stomp around for photos, then invites us in... As usual, all the time is teatime, and there's chocolates left over from the Greek Orthodox Christmas...

TELL US ABOUT THE TREES.

WE WERE SITTING HERE TWO EVENING WHEN WE HEARD A SOUND LIKE A BOMB...

"Somebody was wounded beyond our neighbor's house —a Palestinian who'd been preparing a Molotov cockta He moved into the street and signalled for cars to stop...

"A settler stopped, and then a car driven by a Palestinian. The settler took the ID card of the Palestinian driver and told him to drive the wounded man to the settlement. The settler followed in his car...

"At 4 a.m. the soldiers drove by with loudspeaker and imposed an immediate curfew on the area...

"The following day, in the afternoon, the soldiers returned and cut down the olive trees of my neighbors, the trees along the street...

"The next day they came back and cut my six olive trees...

WHY YOU ARE CRYING?

BECAUSE YOU ARE CUTTING MY TREES.

THAT'S NOTHING.

"The soldiers lifted the curfew...

"All together they cut down 70 olive trees, the trees of 13 families."

And speaking of settlements, Sami drives us to the village outskirts...

ALL THE LAND ON THIS SIDE OF THE ROAD HAS BEEN CONFISCATED BY THE ISRAELIS FOR SETTLEMENT...

It's scores of acres of farmland and pasture we're looking at... again, just drops in the bucket... Israel has expropriated two-thirds of the West Bank for its own use, including the settlement of Jews... (and I'm not counting annexed "Greater Jerusalem")...but like Prime Minister Shamir says:

IF WE ESTABLISH A SETTLEMENT HERE OR EXPAND A SETTLEMENT THERE, THIS IS ONLY NATURAL. WE ARE OPERATING ACCORDING TO THE UNDERSTANDING THAT THE LAND BELONGS TO US.

And with that "understanding" in mind, the World Zionist Organization's 'Master Plan 2010' points out that only five percent of the West Bank is "problematic for settlement..."

I suppose what makes it "problematic" is that hundreds of thousands of Palestinians still live here ... in the countryside, though, they're mostly confined within village boundaries set under British rule in 1942... and the Israelis routinely reject rural building applications, forcing tens of thousands of Palestinians to build and live in "illegal" dwellings, hundreds of which are leveled every year... in fact, according to some official Israeli figures, in '87 and '88 the Israelis demolished more Palestinian homes than they granted building licenses...

But if a Jew wants to join a settlement on occupied Arab land, it's full steam ahead! Incentives to make your head spin! A government grant to offset moving expenses! Eligibility for higher loans at lower interest! Cheaper housing than in Israel! A seven percent income tax deduction! You get the idea — the yuppie version of the Homestead Act...

63

A neighbor who's been listening invites us to his home, which he says was attacked three nights ago...

WE'VE HAD A LONG STORY WITH THE SETTLERS. THE SOLDIERS SAY WE THROW STONES AT THE SETTLERS' CARS. THESE INCIDENTS ARE A REACTION TO THE SETTLERS' BEHAVIOR...

At his home, the front windows are shattered...

Inside, glass and dozens of large stones, left there like the axe, I suppose to prove to visitors—and maybe themselves—that such things happen...

IT WAS ON THE EVE OF OUR GREEK ORTHODOX CHRISTMAS... 10 P.M. ... I WAS SITTING HERE WATCHING T.V....

"A group of cars drove down the main street honking horns. The first car stopped and two settlers got out with guns and fired four times in the air...

GET OUT OF YOUR HOUSES, DOGS!

"...and they yelled bad words about prostitutes—sex words— in Arabic and Hebrew...

"There were nearly 20 cars and maybe 40 settlers, both sexes. I heard a child calling for his father in Hebrew...

65

Before we can digest lunch or anything else, Sami drives us to the next bummer...

...a demolished home.

An old lady invites us in to an adjacent, one-room building...

The kettle's on... more tea!

I HAVE ONE SON IN AMERICA, ONE IN IRAQ—WE HAVEN'T HEARD FROM HIM IN A LONG TIME... MY 26-YEAR-OLD SON IS IN ANSAR III PRISON SERVING A FIVE-YEAR SENTENCE FOR THROWING A MOLOTOV COCKTAIL. HIS WIFE, WHO HAS NO ISRAELI ID, WAS REFUSED REENTRY WHEN SHE TRIED TO GET BACK FROM JORDAN. SHE'S BEEN THERE TWO YEARS...

WE USED TO LIVE IN THE HOUSE: ME, MY SON, AND HIS WIFE.

"One month after he was arrested, the soldiers came and surrounded the house. They told us to leave...

"A bulldozer arrived...

YOU HAVE ARRESTED MY SON! HIS FATHER DIED 20 YEARS AGO!

"We tried immediately to take out the furniture. Many neighbors came to help us. We had one hour, and many things were left inside...

"They told me to get into this room and lock the door, and they demolished our house..."

68

While his trial isn't over, the settler needn't worry unduly about the scales of Israeli justice. From Dec. '87 to Oct. '91, settlers killed 42 Palestinians, and in that time only three trials have concluded. The stiffest sentence? Three years.

On the other hand, Palestinians killed 17 settlers during the same time period. Six of nine suspects captured in these incidents received life imprisonment; one received 20 years; six family homes were demolished. (The remaining two suspects were still in court.)

HOW DO YOU FEEL ABOUT THE SETTLERS?

WHAT KIND OF FEELING WOULD *YOU* HAVE IF YOUR DOOR WAS SMASHED DOWN?

WOULD IT BE A FEELING OF LOVE?

YOU DON'T FEEL SECURE IN YOUR OWN HOME... YOUR OWN STREET...

WHO DO WE HAVE TO COMPLAIN TO? THE SOLDIERS?

Before we go someone hands Saburo a photo of the two dead youths...

Saburo doesn't say a thing the whole drive back. In Jerusalem he says he doesn't want the photo...

TOO HEAVY... TOO HEAVY...

And after a day like today, sure it's too heavy, even for a vulture like me. But—

I'LL TAKE IT.

'cause faces are what it's all about, man...

...and I put the faces way in the bottom of my pack...

...I mean, who's to say they'll be too heavy tomorrow?

71

J. SACCO 3-93

WHERE IS SABURO?

For two days, three, I wait. News of more curfews and the downpours keep me in Jerusalem...

Where is he, dammit?

What's he seeing?

All I've done is get three or four chicken-shit interviews and watch the border police check IDs at Damascus Gate...

Finally Saburo comes back, his shoes muddy... Last time I saw him, the taxi had dropped him off at Balata camp ...From there he walked to Camp One, he says, where the soldiers had just sealed the house of a suspect and were popping tear gas to disperse a crowd... Later an angry Palestinian took him by the hand, wanted to show him something...

A BABY. HEAD VERY LARGE. THEY SAY MOTHER WHEN PREGNANT BECOMES SICK FROM TEAR GAS.

I'm a skeptic. Journalistically speaking, you gotta be a Doubting Thomas; you gotta make sure. It's good to get your finger in the wound. Your whole head would be better.

DID YOU GET A PICTURE?

OF THE BABY?

I DON'T WANT TAKE PICTURE, BUT THEY WANT ME TAKE PICTURE.

AND?

I TAKE PICTURE... VERY HARD.

Man, I wish I'd seen the soldiers firing tear gas...

wish I'd seen that baby.

J. SACCO 4-93

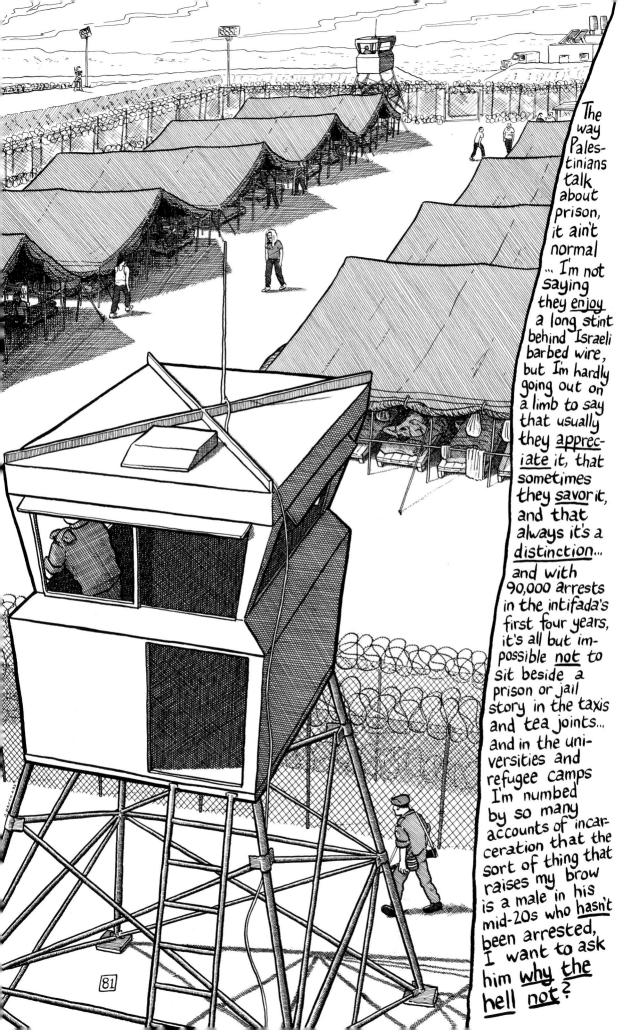

The way Palestinians talk about prison, it ain't normal ... I'm not saying they enjoy a long stint behind Israeli barbed wire, but I'm hardly going out on a limb to say that usually they appreciate it, that sometimes they savor it, and that always it's a distinction... and with 90,000 arrests in the intifada's first four years, it's all but impossible not to sit beside a prison or jail story in the taxis and tea joints... and in the universities and refugee camps I'm numbed by so many accounts of incarceration that the sort of thing that raises my brow is a male in his mid-20s who hasn't been arrested, I want to ask him why the hell not?

81

Don't get me wrong, I'm not about to trivialize the Palestinian prison experience... It's just that getting locked up is such an integral part of life here that I resignedly anticipate the subject coming up _somehow_ (no matter whom I'm talking to), in _someway_ (whether in detail or just in passing)...

But even I had to crack a smile that time in a West Bank village when an easygoing fellow introduced me to his typically large brood, including a pretty girl with a pretty name...

ANSAR, SHAKE HANDS.

Ansar

Ansar

Ansar

And her father didn't have to tell me _if_ or _where_ he'd done _his_ time, 'cause there's a prison in the desert called...

ANSAR III

There are other prisons, of course, but Ansar III, which the Israelis call Ketziot, is the largest, holding 6,000 inmates as of Nov. '91. It opened in March '88 specifically to deal with the intifada overflow...

I've spoken to plenty of Ansar III alumni, but the recollections that follow are drawn from interviews with three whose stories seem typical...

Yusef

Mohammed

Iyyad

Each is a middle-aged professional who was held in administrative detention...

Administrative detention is six months' imprisonment imposed without trial...

It can be renewed for an additional six months... and then another six months ... and then again... and

I'd tell you what crimes these men committed but none was charged with any...

Be that as it may...

YOU FALL INTO THE TRAP OF TRYING TO FIGUR OUT WHA YOU DID WRON

Our stories begin following Yusef's arrest in March '88 as he arrived at Dhahriya prison, south of Hebron in the West Bank, which also was Iyyad's starting point...

"It was during the Iron Fist period, during the policy of 'broken bones.' We were blind-folded and hand-cuffed and they beat us on the bus. When we got out we had to pass between two lines of soldiers who beat us. Two prisoners had arms broken. Then they ordered us to make animal noises and noises like a train. They beat us until we agreed to do this. Soldiers were having a barbeque nearby, including women soldiers."

The first two days at Dhahriya I spent under the sky... Then I spent 11 days in a cell. There were 35 of us. There was a barrel toilet and it was full. We told the soldiers, but it was during the night and raining so they didn't want to empty it right then. A fat prisoner had to go. He climbed onto the toilet, lost his balance, and the whole thing tipped over.

"The room was full of shit. We were shouting. We carried our shoes in our hands and our socks in our shoes. The soldiers came after half an hour, and they gave us soap and water to clean with, but we spent five days with the smell."

"I spent 18 days at Dhahriya before receiving an administrative detention order for six months. I was placed in a room of 4×6 meters with about 40 persons. In ten days they allowed us out of the room only twice, for 15 minutes each time."

SACCO 4-93

"I was moved to a tent for two or three days, which was much better, but then they moved me to another room, which I considered a sort of hell. I remained in this room for a week. It was 3×4 meters, with 21 persons. The metal door faced the sun from noon on. The ventilation was very bad, just a coin-sized hole in the door for injecting gas in case of a riot.

"For ventilation, two people would take a blanket and flap it up and down. We did this in ten-minute shifts.

"I did not sleep more than two to three hours a night maximum. I'd sit on the rubbish bin with my nose against the hole until I fell asleep from exhaustion."

The first prisoners to be transferred to Ansar III didn't know where they were being taken. Yusef was among them...

"They took us from our rooms and they put us on five buses. There were more than 100 of us. We were afraid. Some were crying on the buses. We thought we were being deported to Jordan or Lebanon.

J. SACCO 5·93

84

"After about four hours they took us off the buses and we found ourselves in front of tents. We knew nothing of our location or why they had put us there."

"I spoke to a Druze soldier who told me this was a new prison."

"They ordered us to take off our clothes and to put on dark blue uniforms. On the first night we were each given one piece of bread, five olives, and a spoonful of jam."

"They also gave each of us three blankets and a thin mattress. It was very cold in the tents. I couldn't sleep."

We felt like animals," Yusef said, and he added a specific or two to the list of privations I'd already collected from other ex-prisoners: the desert temperature extremes; the insects; a water supply so insufficient it had to be utilized almost exclusively for drinking; a bland, inadequate diet; no change of clothes; little medical care... enough stuff, in other words, for another comics series... but let's not get bogged down by the summed-behind-barbed-wire material 'cause, anyway, some things have improved with time and pressure... water, for example, is more readily available... writing implements are allowed, newspapers, too... and in Oct. '91 — three and a half years after Ansar III opened for business — regular family visits were arranged. In the meantime, the prison expanded to keep up with the growing number of intifada arrests...

"I was in the first section, Section A. After ten days the section was full. One month later they built Section B, and a month after that, Section C.... The next time I was arrested, in Jan. 1990, Ansar III seemed like a city to me."

"I was in Section H, subsection 2. Subsection 2 was divided into four units. Each unit had three tents, with 25 people to a tent."

85

"Out of the five subsections, two were called cages. Each unit in a cage was surrounded by prefabricated cement walls, with an iron net on top. A prisoner in a cage would see nothing but three tents, the walls, and the sky. The cages were used to isolate leaders and activists."

"We communicated with other sections by throwing messages tied to stones or pieces of dried bread. These were called 'post-balls' or the 'fax.'"

According to Yusef, the prisoners—who included doctors, teachers, lawyers, and journalists —soon began discussing ways of organizing themselves...

"In the first day we didn't have any organiza-tion. We wanted order. Our first success was forming one line for the W.C."

"Being stuck in a yard with 250 guys might seem like hell to some people, with only three toilets and hot water once every three weeks.... We were in charge of distributing our food ourselves, and there was only one plate for every four detainees... so we had to be organized. We formed committees to organize these things."

A couple of examples of h these committ function migh prove instruct and naturally my ears prick up when Mohammed me tioned somethi called "the te committee"....

86

"Prisoners working in the kitchen would bring the tea in a big pot. The tea committee had to make sure that distribution of the tea was fair, so that no one complained, and fast, so that the tea was served hot.

"The tea committee served everyone once, and then began serving from the beginning of the line again until the leftover was gone. The tea monitor in the tent would take note of who was next in line for tea so that he would be first served next time.

"There's a problem the moment you start goofing with fairness. Prison is a small world where a cup of tea is something, a piece of soap is something."

And as for edifying activities...

"If we wanted to gather for a talk, the education committee would decide on the speakers, which tent, and how many people could attend.... A few people would be sent to walk along the barbed wire to take the attention of the guards elsewhere.... We held lectures on ecology, philosophy, Einstein, the break-up of the Soviet Union...."

"Twice I lectured on the Israeli peace movement."

"There were courses in English and Hebrew. In three months 14 persons were taught how to read."

"Ansar is our university," a student in Bethlehem once told me, and he added a story so tidy I chalked it up to apocrypha (but who knows?): A Bir Zeit University professor was sent to Ansar III and found himself in the same tent as some of his students—so he continued his course and even administered an exam...

Besides lectures and studies, Yusef said, prisoners put on skits that demonstrated Israeli interrogation methods and on one occasion a play that dramatized the death of a Palestinian in custody...

"The play was under three tents we had joined together. At the end, everyone clapped, and the soldiers fired tear gas."

All the activities and organizational structures mentioned here, as well as prison discipline, were controlled by political committees representing the various factions of the PLO — Fateh, the Popular Front, the Democratic Front, the Communists, etc.

"Every new prisoner entering the compound had to affiliate himself with a faction — not for political reasons, but for purposes of organization. This did not imply he was a member of that group... but he had to answer to the group for certain responsibilities, and the group became responsible for his rights and duties.

"No one was allowed to speak to new prisoners when they came in, so there would be no question of recruiting. The prisoner would be taken to a tent where a committee of four would ask him to choose a political faction.... The only disadvantage to this system was that it was highly centralized."

The extent of prisoner solidarity, despite diverse political views, is well demonstrated by an event that took place early in the history of Ansar III...

"I hid the newspaper and took it to a friend from Jenin who could read Hebrew. When he read it he began crying."

THEY'VE KILLED ABU JIHAD*!

"I worked in the kitchen with three others. We used to take the rubbish from the kitchen to dump with the soldiers' rubbish, and I found a Hebrew newspaper in there.

* Abu Jihad (Khalil Al-Wazir) – formed the Palestinian revolutionary group Fateh with his close friend Yasser Arafat. Assassinated by Israeli commandoes in Tunis, April 16, 1988. "We were one spirit in two bodies," Arafat said of him.

As part of the kitchen staff distributing food, Yusef helped spread the news, which was already six days old...

Abu Jihad belonged to Fateh, but the other factions wanted to commemorate him, too. Section A's political committee decided to pay tribute to him the next morning...

"We spoke with prisoners and told them what we had learned ...slowly, slowly, so not to start a riot."

"We weren't allowed watches, so we decided to leave our tents during prayers.... After the third 'Allah Aqbar' all of us went out and stood in line for one minute.

J. SACCO 5-93

89

"The administration was very nervous. A lot of soldiers appeared with automatic weapons... tanks started up, sending up sand.... They ordered us over loudspeakers to get into our tents. Then they started shooting in the sky and throwing tear gas.... The prisoners started throwing stones, their shoes. In the kitchen we were throwing onions. It was an half-hour riot. Some prisoners were wounded by rubber bullets, but the Israelis received our message."

"If you want to achieve something, you have to know how far you can push the authorities. If we started singing nationalistic or folk songs, for example, the soldiers were authorized to tell us to stop.

SHUT UP!

"We ignore him, and he might tell us three times. He tells an officer, and the officer comes to warn our subsection, next time there might be tear gas. As soon as we see it's serious, we stop.... Half an hour later we start up again."

Prisoners also learned to accommodate their activities to the schedules of the guards, determining when the Israelis were more likely to let things slide...

"We knew on Thursdays it was better because the commander went home, and he didn't want to spend the night for a disturbance."

Also, the lecture schedule was "usually intensified during the final days of the soldiers' duty when they were less likely to interfere," according to Mohammed...

"The soldiers rotate every 15 days. At first they have stereotypes about the prisoners. They act tough. They watch out for 'postballs' and make searches.... After seven or ten days they see things differently, they're impressed with our organization. The moment they start to relax and act as humans, we have about three days with them ...and then we get another bunch of bastards."

"The last time I was in Ansar III, I had good relations with some soldiers. I talked to an American Israeli who told me he was surprised by our conditions, but he couldn't refuse to serve."

"And I had a friend who used to work in Haifa, and after three months in Ansar his old boss, a Jew, ended up being one of the guards. He gave my friend some cigarettes."

J. SACCO · 6·93

"Getting to know the guards isn't so much a way of easing conditions. We want to counteract the policy of recruiting Israelis to be Palestinian-haters."

"Look at how it works, this fucking Israeli guard duty. It serves the ideological purpose of exposing Israelis to conditions where they don't see Palestinians as humans.... They see people, first of all, dressed like animals, who, until recently, didn't have spoons to eat with... people who are dirty, who have no access to proper hygiene, with hundreds of different flies and mosquitoes around their faces. And it sticks in their minds — 'Those are my enemies'.... Soviet Jews who've never seen a Palestinian are taken to serve in detention camps and in the occupied territories. They can learn to be haters, too.

"Ansar III wasn't set up just to counteract the intifada; it's also a policy.... The same faces keep showing up in the prisons, so it's not a deterrence."

As their confinement comes to an end, prisoners often have one last obligation to the comrades they're leaving behind —getting messages to friends and loved ones on the outside...

"It's the usual routine.... You swallow capsules with messages. They're plastic with the ends melted to form a seal.... I swallowed at least 14 such messages. On the day you are released, people come up to you and ask if you have a message for them. You say, "Yes, but maybe tomorrow.""

The first time he was released from Ansar III, Yusef told me, was the happiest moment of his life. Many people, journalists, came to greet him. When the Israelis arrested him again, four months later, he was here in his office, where we sipped tea...

I DON'T CARE IF THEY ARREST ME. I DON'T WANT TO BE IN PRISON AGAIN, BUT THIS IS OUR LIFE.

WHAT CAN WE DO EXCEPT CONTINUE THE STRUGGLE?

J. SACCO 5-93

And the stories don't get much better than that... they're vulgar stuff for behind the shed ...stylistically, speaking, disappointing...

which isn't to say the interrogations themselves aren't effective... 'cause Abid, for example, who whispered how he'd been left naked in cold cells, who was beaten with clubs and strangled, who had his balls stomped, he signed a confession...

...ut when he ...etracted his confession in ...ourt, the Shin Bet denied touching him... "We brought him tea and coffee," he told me they told the court...

And Abid got 15 years...

Sure it's worse somewhere else... it always is, isn't it? But we're talking about Israel now, "the Middle East's only democracy," and this kind of thing troubled the Israelis, too, so in '87 the government commissioned a retired supreme court president, Justice Moshe Landau, to investigate...

The Landau report determined, indeed, that Shin Bet officers consistently had lied in court by denying they'd extracted confessions through physical force... and, incidentally, the report recommended that no charges be brought against those responsible...

And the Landau report reasoned that, in the interest of defending Israel from "terrorist activity," the Shin Bet must be allowed some means of "non-violent psychological pressure" and "moderate...physical pressure" in its interrogations... Just what constituted such permissible pressure was outlined in Part II of the report, which has been kept secret... but rest assured that it included (in the report's wording) nothing "disproportionate," nothing on the "level of physical torture," nothing that "deprives [a suspect] of his human dignity...."

So Justice Landau got the Israel Prize and Israel goes on being "the Middle East's only democracy"... and Palestinians go on being interrogated, though now within secret guidelines, subject to who-knows-what interpretations, and, whatever else you want to say about the "new" methods, now they're legal...

Some time later the door opened, the air revived her...

YOU'RE NOT DEAD YET?

I WANT TO VOMIT.

And they tied her and hooded her —the Palestinians call this technique "Al-Shabah"— "sometimes four hours, sometimes the whole day... sometimes they take you in the middle of the night for this."

They made her sit up straight with a metal bar pressing down the center of her back, she says, they hit her when she leaned against the wall...

But worst of all was isolation, her cell, which was besmirched with filth, she says, and where she was left without toilet paper and sanitary napkins...

She longed for the interrogations, when she'd have someone to talk to... "I'd have fun with them"... she says she'd figured out the Shin Bet...

"They have some information against you. First they want you to confirm the information. Second, they want you to provide additional information, to implicate others..."

The Shin Bet reckoned they could play the twin cards of gender and Arab culture against her... They implied a long imprisonment would ruin her marriage prospects...

WE DON'T ARREST GIRLS. WE KNOW YOUR SITUATION AS A GIRL IN YOUR SOCIETY. NO ONE WILL MARRY YOU.

IN 25 YEARS I'LL BE OUT, THEY'LL BE STANDING IN LINE FOR ME, BUT YOU MAY BE DEAD.

98

It's a wet February day, a day of bullhorns and chants for a "martyr"...

A wonder the Israelis are permitting such a demonstrative funeral procession... I suppose it's time to let the Palestinians blow off a little patriotic steam...

I've run into Saleh, my photographer buddy from the wire service, and he's checking out the breeze and fields of fire, he's sure there'll be gas, an attack...

LAST TIME, I LOST CONSCIOUS- NESS... THEY HAD TO CARRY ME OUT...

But the Israelis hold back even when several youths, masked and asking for it, further risk their necks to plant an illegal Palestinian flag from the Al-Aqsa mosque... and as the crowd cheers, it seems Mustafa is merely the footnote to a defiant day...

J. SACCO 6-93

Make no mistake, everywhere you go, not just in Marvel Comics, there's parallel universes... Here? On the surface streets: traffic, couples in love, falafel-to-go, tourists in jogging suits licking stamps for postcards... And over the wall behind closed doors: other things — people strapped to chairs, sleep deprivation, the smell of piss... other things happening for "reasons of national security" ...for "security reasons"...to combat "terrorist activity"...they were happening to Ghassan a week and a half ago, he shows me his back and wrists, he's still got the marks... he's a fresh case, all right ... right off the rack...

'MODERATE PRESSURE' PART 2

Now he's back in his middle class living room in East Jerusalem offering tea and goodies to a guest...Four weeks ago he was a suspect, arrested in the same sweep that got Mustafa Akkawi — remember him? — the guy we just buried...

Ghassan tells me his story, his kids climbing all over him.

And soon his little girl is fast asleep... Probably she's too young to understand, or else she's heard it all before... in any case, she's asleep...

And sleep is where Ghassan's story starts... where stories like this always start... when people are asleep...

And then the door gets bashed down...

"One time I heard someone talking. I felt once the police come and hit someone.

"Tapes were playing from speakers...very loud... Hebrew songs, English, some Arabic.

"They played three or four cassettes, the same songs, 24 hours a day.

ARE YOU READY TO TALK NOW?

"After about 30 hours from my arrest, the police came for me.

"I felt this time they'll take me to court.

"They took the sack from my head and untied me and left me four or five hours in an office.

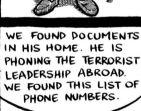

"My hands were swollen. The color of my skin was reddish blue.

"I was taken to a court. My lawyer was present but I wasn't allowed to speak to him.

YOUR HONOR, WE BELIEVE THE SUSPECT BELONGS TO AN ILLEGAL ORGANIZATION.

THAT'S NOT TRUE. WHAT EVIDENCE DO YOU HAVE?

WE FOUND DOCUMENTS IN HIS HOME. HE IS PHONING THE TERRORIST LEADERSHIP ABROAD. WE FOUND THIS LIST OF PHONE NUMBERS.

THIS IS THE NUMBER OF MY BROTHER-IN-LAW, OTHER RELATIVES OF MY WIFE..., WHERE I WORK... A HOSPITAL... NUMBERS OF MY RELATIVES...

"The judge could read Arabic. He looked at the list himself.

YOUR HONOR, WE NEED 15 MORE DAYS TO FIND ADDITIONAL EVIDENCE.

YOUR HONOR, THERE IS NO EVIDENCE. MY CLIENT SHOULD BE RELEASED IMMEDIATELY.

Chapter Five

get an
tline,
alf in
nglish,
alf in
antomime:
Settlers
attacked
yesterday,
four people
shot...

one here

another
here

one here

THEY COME
WITH CHILDREN,
WITH WOMEN!
FIVE WOMEN!
TEN!

These two, in
fact, they're
on their way
to Jerusalem
to see their
buddy in hos-
pital, the one
who got it in
the head...

where's a taxi?

meanwhile, I'm a jour-
nalist, a professional,
I need more details...
Okay, this fellow knows
someone who's got better
English, this way please...

I'm introduced to Bassem, he's
closing up his shop for now, he'll
take me to his cousin. I tell
him I want the facts, the
story on yesterday's attack...

A customer shrugs...

SOMETHING
ALWAYS HAPPENS.
YESTERDAY IN
HEBRON, TODAY
SOMEWHERE ELSE,
BUT SOMETHING
ALWAYS HAPPENS...

assem leads
e up a few
reets... in
small work-
hop he intro-
uces me to
hafeek, a
tudent at
lebron's uni-
ersity...

The place fills
up with young
men, kids
from the
neighborhood,
piles of them...
I tell you, I
could pack
bleachers at
some of my
interviews,
clean up on
a tea con-
cession...

okay, every-
one's nice
'n' cozy? now
what about
yesterday's
attack?

I CAME TO MY
HOME. I SAW TWO
CARS CARRYING
THE INJURED. THE
SOLDIERS CAME
TWO OR THREE HOURS
LATER AND IMPOSED
A CURFEW...

That's it? But this is
second-hand info...
he heard shots but
didn't see any
shooting...

Obviously I'm getting nowhere on this attack story... the talk shifts to the occupation in general, the prospect for peace....

I SUPPORT PEACE, BUT I DON'T BELIEVE IT WILL HAPPEN... WHEN ISRAEL TALKS OF PEACE IT IS BECAUSE OF AMERICAN PRESSURE... AND THE AL-HUSSEIN MISSILES FROM IRAQ!

YOU MEAN DURING THE GULF WAR? THE SCUDS?

NO! THEY WERE NOT SCUDS! THEY WERE AL-HUSSEIN MISSILES, MADE IN IRAQ!!

okay okay, made in Iraq!

WE WERE HAPPY SEEING THE ISRAELIS DESTROYED BY THE MISSILES... WE WERE ON THE ROOF SAYING, "ALLAH AQBAR!" MY NEIGHBOR HERE WAS BEATEN FOR CHEERING THE MISSILES THEY BEAT HIS BROTHERS TOO, EVEN THE ONES NOT ON THE ROOF...

WE DON'T WANT TO SEE ANYONE KILLED, BUT THE JEWS KILL US AND THE MISSILES KILL THE JEWS, AND THAT MAKES US HAPPY!

Yikes! These guys could use the service of a good public relations officer.

I mean, it's the turn-the-other-cheek stuff that gets out the knitting circle...

But I've heard this business before... in Beit Sahour an old woman told me she'd "enjoyed" the missile attacks, she'd welcomed Saddam Hussein's promise to liberate Palestine. "When you are drowning," she said, "you grab anything to stay afloat, even the tiniest piece of wood."

And as for Shafeek...

I AM COMPLETELY SYMPATHETIC WITH IRAQ. SADDAM HUSSEIN IS OUR FINAL HOPE. NOW HE IS TRYING TO REBUILD HIS POWER, HIS ARMY.

Time to shift gears again... I want to know about Hebron... Thousands of Jews have settled nearby since the '70s, some forcibly in the heart of town... Are there any relations between settlers and Palestinians in Hebron?

THERE ARE NO RELATIONS, ONLY HOSTILE RELATIONS! BOTH SIDES HATE EACH OTHER!

That answers that question! And I suppose it'd be too much to expect any Palestinian lipstick on settlers' collars in this burg! Or vice versa! This is an eye-for-an-eye town...

March '79: Two Palestinian teenagers killed.
Jan. '80: Soldier-yeshiva student shot dead.
May '80: Six yeshiva students killed after prayers.
Nov. '81: After one Jew is stabbed, three Palestinian children are shot.
March '82: Two Palestinians killed, seven wounded.
Oct. '82: Two Palestinian children wounded in grenade attack.
July '83: Yeshiva student killed; machine-gun and grenade attack on Islamic College kills three Palestinian students.

You get the picture, the list goes on... but let's skip it for now, lunch is being served...

"When they got into the street, they attacked homes and caused damage. They threw stones at the windows...

"Women and children began screaming, calling for help...

"People came and began throwing stones at them, and the settlers began shooting in all directions...

"One of those injured was trying to close his shop. He was trying to get his things inside. The people wounded were passing by, not the ones throwing stones."

THE SETTLERS RAN TO THE CENTER OF THE CITY AND THE PEOPLE FOLLOWED...

THE SOLDIERS CAME TO PROTECT THE SETTLERS...

And so we can add another line t our unhappy list... we've had some more tit-for-tat in Hebron, and I exp it'll be tat again before too long...

Anyway, the next morning I pick up the Israeli English-language daily and get a different slant on the settlers' armed family outing in the Palestinian neighborhood...

THE JERUSALEM POST 60 1932-1992

Vol. LX, No. 17960 Sunday, January 26, 1992 • Shvat 21, 5752 • Rajab 21, 1412 NIS 2.90 (Eilat NIS 2.50)

major factor in d.....
for elections.

...in aims for

...housewives .
government legalized all private ...sactions, ...

Seven hurt in Hebron shooting incident

Three Kiryat Arba residents were lightly injured and four Hebron Arabs critically, seriously, and lightly hurt in an incident yesterday afternoon.

A group of Jewish families, members of the Kach-affiliated Committee for Safety on the Roads, were patrolling in the Harat a-Sheikh section of Hebron, when they were attacked by several hundred Arabs. They said they were pelted with rocks and bottles from rooftops and alleys.

Two children and a woman were injured.

Two escape, the settlers fired in the air, and when that had no effect, they said they fired at the legs of the rock-throwers.

Last night, four wounded Arabs were brought to Mokassad Hospital in East Jerusalem. One, the hospital reported, was in critical condition with a bullet wound in the abdomen. Two others were seriously wounded in the head and chest, and a third lightly wounded in the leg.

The IDF relayed a report on the incident to the Hebron police, who have opened an investigation.

The Committee for Safety on the Roads said it would continue to patrol Arab neighborhoods which Jews have previously preferred not to enter.

On Friday, some 150 settlers from Kiryat Arba and Hebron had blocked the road to Kiryat Arba where it passes through the Tark section of Hebron. They charged that cars and buses were constantly being stoned there.

After two hours, the IDF convinced the settlers to open the road.

(Itim)

Moslem fundamentalists

WOMEN

I have an appointment, seven o'clock, I'm here to get the lowdown on the Palestinian women's movement... Sorry, I'm told, I'm meant for a wait... Meanwhile, there's a loud discussion in the next room...

ten minutes it lasts...

then a teenaged girl and her mother make their exit...

My turn, I'm ushered in...

I meet a couple of executive members of the Palestinian Federation of Women's Action Committees...

They fill me in...

The girl who left, she's 15 years old, her second marriage is on the rocks ...She's got a baby from her first marriage, she was 14 back then and knew nothing about the responsibility of building a family... At the first sign of problems: divorce!

Two months later she married again, Husband Number Two beat her, he wanted her to go buy tea, there were soldiers outside and she refused, he threw hot water on her...

She went back to her mother's in Nablus, left her gold jewelry and furniture at Hubby Number Two's in Hebron...

He wants her to waive her right to the stuff, to relinquish any financial claims... She's not sure of the legalities, she came for advice...

J. SACCO 10·93

e says Islam nd the vast jority of Pal- tinian women e Muslim— ants women operty rights, nd Islamic w can be terpreted to e advantage f women... arriage con- racts, for xample, are a feature of Islam...

"A woman get- ting married can put condi- tions on her husband, and if these are not met, she can ask for a divorce... A woman might stipulate that if her husband takes a second wife, that is grounds for a divorce, or if he prevents her from work- ng or leaves o go abroad..."

Polygamy, she says, can be curtailed by a strict reading of Islamic law, which says a man must treat each wife equally — all but an impossibility, she argues...

So, in theory, Islam offers avenues by which women can press for their rights...

BUT IN PRACTICE, THIS IS A GREAT DIF- FICULTY...

And we're back to square one, raising the pol- itical self-awareness of women in the context of certain cultural and rel- igious realities...

Rita is philo- sophical about the slow road to societal change...

LOOK, I'M A CATHOLIC... THREE YEARS AGO I WAS ALL FOR SECULAR LAWS TO PROTECT WOMEN, I WOULDN'T GIVE THE IDEA UP, BUT WE CAN'T ACHIEVE THAT NOW...

Muna, a non-practising Muslim, is more skeptical about using Islamic law to advance women's rights... she sees some irrecon- cilable differences...

WE HAVE A BIG PROBLEM WITH BATTERED WOMEN... THE KORAN PERMITS A MAN TO BEAT A WOMAN ...WOMEN HERE ARE TAUGHT THEY CAN BE SLAPPED, EVEN THE CHRISTIANS... IT'S PART OF THE ARAB CULTURE... WOMEN HERE DON'T COMPLAIN, THEY DON'T CALL THEM- SELVES BATTERED... AND IT'S NOT JUST A CHAR- ACTERISTIC OF THE POOR...

EDUCATE MEN? WE'RE NOT DOING ENOUGH TO EDUCATE WOMEN !

135

J. SACCO 10-93

"We talk about homes for battered women, but you can't just take a woman out of her house here... This is not a rebellion culture... Men, even liberal ones, would react against this... Trying to reconcile, the couple, that's the man's view..."

Feminists need to discuss this and other issues, but the different women's groups correspond to one PLO faction or another and are divided along political lines...

"We clash the nation agenda. We'not working the social agenda together. We're not utilizing common ground. We're not exploiting the PLO constitution which granted women equality with men... We don't have a clear women's agenda..."

All the feminists I met talked of the need to push their views while also resisting the occupation...

And while the revolutionary atmospher of the intifada fosters discussion of soci change, no one's under any illusions about where the women's movement stands in the scheme of things...

Feminists here talk about the lesson of the Algerian revolution, where women fought alongside men but were pushed back into traditional roles once the French were defeated...

IF WE GET A STATE, DO WE RETREAT BACK TO THE WAY THINGS WERE, OR DO WE CHANGE THINGS? WILL ECONOMIC DEVELOPMENT BE CONSIDERED PRIORITY AND WOMEN'S ISSUES LEFT BEHIND?

WE'RE ATTACHED TO THE NATIONAL MOVEMENT...

ANY REGRESSION IN THE NATIONAL MOVEMENT AND WE'RE THE HARDEST HIT PEOPLE...

THE INTIFADA ISN'T OVER BUT PEOPLE FIGURE, "IF W LOSE PALESTI WHY WORRY ABOUT WOMEN?"

136

J. SACCO 10-93

The way Muna tells the story, at the beginning of the uprising the Unified Leadership—which includes the main PLO factions—called for traditional dress as a way of emphasizing Palestinian identity...

Hamas, the extremist Islamic group which rivals the secular PLO, then called for the compulsory wearing of the hijab. She says Hamas followers began threatening women and sometimes beating them for going outside without a head covering...

In Dec. 1990 a first-of-its-kind conference on the social problems of Palestinian women declared women should have the right to choose whether to wear the hijab or not... She says the Unified Leadership concurred with a leaflet and messages saying anyone who attacked a woman for not wearing the hijab was a traitor...

In any case, in the week I spent in the Gaza Strip, where Hamas is particularly strong, not once did I see a woman past her mid-teens outdoors without her head covered...

What am I supposed to think? That Hamas makes them do it?

I meet with a few Gazan women to get some handle on the subject... The first two, ages 19 and 20, live just outside Jabalia refugee camp and say they've worn the hijab since their early teens...

WE BELIEVE WE HAVE TO. AFTER SIX YEARS OF WEARING IT, IT SEEMS LIKE A HABIT TO ME...

IT IS WRITTEN IN THE KORAN.

Well, I should add some Muslim feminists dispute the interpretation of the relevant passages.

J. SACCO 11-93

138

And Hamas?

HAMAS CONSIDERS THE INTIFADA A WAY OF SPREADING ITS AGENDA. THEY WANT TO FORCE WOMEN TO WEAR THE HIJAB...

"One day I was doing some shopping on Omar el-Mukhtar Street. I saw a lady physician driving her car, right by the hospital. She wasn't wearing the hijab. Three or four youths began stoning her car, injuring her, she was bleeding..."

COVER YOUR HEAD!

COVER YOUR HEAD!

WHAT ARE YOU DOING? SHE IS A CHRISTIAN!

At the begin of the intifa Palestinian Christians in wore the hijab be on the safe side, she says not so much She says suc violent activiti against wome have decrease

TOP-COLA

In the same office, two attractive young women, decked out with cosmetics, seem to counter everything I've seen in Gaza thusfar...

I SEE YOU'RE NOT WEARING THE HIJAB.

WE WEAR IT OUTSIDE.

So, do they feel obliged to wear it?

No no no! I've got it all wrong! On the contrary—

I WANT TO BELIEVE STRONGLY ENOUGH TO WEAR THE HIJAB ALWAYS...

Did I catch that right?

NOT JUST IN THE STREET. I WANT TO REALLY BELIE IN WEARING IT...

I tell you, that throws me for a loop, and I see the gulf between us...

I realize then I've forgotten what it's like to have faith...

I mean, I've forgotten what it's like to want to have faith...

140

Chapter Six

...and if you don't ask them to stop, they'll stop anyway beneath the orange and white tower that rises from the Israeli Defense Forces base and watches unblinkingly over Jabalia refugee camp...

...'cause they'll have something else to show you, they'll want to conclude your UNRWA outing on an upbeat note, it's not all open sewage and omniscient IDF towers in Jabalia, you know...

...they'll take you into the rehab center where deaf kids are taught to speak... the class will stop for you, and a teacher will trot out the star pupil... he's deaf like a nail but he can read lips...

FUQ.

FUQ!

He'll write it on the board, too...

See!

Three cheers!

Progress is being made!

فوق

149

ROOMS

That's the Mediterranean rising up

The towers, that's the prison for Palestinians, Ansar II

J. SACCO 12.93

Nuseirat refugee camp, Block 2

It's been raining

Once, when I was shuddering at conditions in Balata camp on the West Bank, someone told me, "If you think this is bad, you should see Gaza."

So I saw Gaza, sort of... I did the UNRWA tour, in and out in two hours.

And I did Gaza by numbers... 140 square miles (I read), three-quarters of a million Palestinians, one of the most densely populated areas on earth ... 70 percent registered as refugees... almost 300,000 in eight UNRWA-administered camps (like this one)... per capita income of $1,700, one-ninth of that in Israel... 40 percent unemployment... and so on, I sloshed through the dozens of this and millions of that...

150

This visit, I'm with Larry, an American who teaches English in Gaza Town...

We've just spent a pleasant mid-day in his apartment, not a bad place, he made a lentil soup lunch, afterwards we sat around with Nescafés and advanced our respective theories... You know the sort of conversation, one that gallops from this to that smoothly and beautifully... the Nature of God, the State of the American Left, Zionism, whatever... He opened the Koran, I paraphrased Orwell, and fondly we recalled Chomsky we had read...

But now we're in the mud.

He says he's got pals up here, just a few more puddles to go.

A door opens...

You come to someone's house, you enter through the door, you expect a hallway or front room...

But none of that here, no roof, no floor even, just sand...

J. SACCO 12-93

151

Someone's showing me his permit to work in Israel, he's doctored it, see? He's extended his permit by scratching off a zero. "He does it because he must work," someone explains, "The Israelis take so long to renew his papers"... Nuseirat camp, the Gaza Strip, unemployment 40 percent, a job in Israel is a prized thing even though

the average daily wage for Palestinian workers is just $20, even if transportation to work costs more than half that, even if it means four hours travelling time to and from Tel Aviv every day... This guy's a lucky one, too, he works, he teaches locally, over in Khan Younis... What's his name again? Masud? Masud. Masud who teaches

in Khan Younis... He tells me why the school, <u>two</u> schools, were closed in Nuseirat yesterday. What happened? "The soldiers come," he says, "two Thursdays in a row, they park near the school. It's a provocation and someone throws a stone. The soldiers go in with tear gas, shooting rubber and live bullets." Once, Masud says, a student

where he teaches, an eight year old, was killed by a rubber bullet, it entered the boy's head... The Gaza Strip, lots of kids get shot here... in '89, for example, of 3,779 live-round casualties, 1,506 were children under 15, 33 were five years old or younger... Masud, though, doesn't seem too bitter. So, does he have hopes for peace with Israel? "No," he says, "I have no hope. Things won't change." But that seems almost beside the point to Masud. "We Arabs have tried nationalism," he says, "but what the people must do is return to their Muslim roots. Fundamentalism is on the rise and that's a good thing. Now it is the turn of Islam." The turn of Islam?

Fundamentalism? That's the cue for all true white men to form a perimeter around the women and children!... But Masud's brand of fundamentalism doesn't sound like the militancy of Hamas, the resistance movement which emphasizes a forceful liberation of Palestine as it moves to Islamize Palestinian society. And someone—

his name is Ibrahim, and this is his room, I take it, his couch — says <u>he</u> believes in the armed struggle all right. "The Israelis only understand force," he says. How? What force? "There are ways. So far it's been stones, but there are guns." Yes yes, I've heard this before, Palestinians stewing in rooms like this one, raising a finger in

warning and the specter of shooting Israelis... The intifada thus far, they say, has been an exercise in restraint... But the Israelis are exponentially more powerful than the Palestinians, does Ibrahim expect a hand (or a tank corps) from the Arab states? "The other Arabs are worthless," he says. "They're talk talk talk. Where was

Qaddafi during the Gulf War? Only Saddam Hussein attacked Israel. He kept his word. Was he a man or was he a man?" Ibrahim's on a roll now about Palestinian military prowess, his commando raid Top Ten... Did I hear about the shebab who seized the bus and made a seven-kilometer run attacking Israeli positions until a

helicopter got them? And what about Leila Khaled?! A PFLP guerilla, she helped hijack those airliners to Jordan, the ones blown up after being emptied of passengers and crew... "I don't agree with those tactics," says a man with a beard. "They didn't get us anywhere." And Masud, the fundamentalist, agrees... Probably they've talked this

through a hundred times before in Nuseirat, in other camps, in villages and towns, in rooms just like this one, with the tea coming and coming, year after year... And it was a young man from Nuseirat, married, with a newborn baby, and one of the lucky ones, too, with a job, who forced an Israeli bus into a

ravine, killing 15, and he wasn't under orders from Fateh or the PFLP or Hamas, his was a personal explosion, maybe he'd been dwelling on his best friend, whose spine had been cut through by an Israeli bullet... And someone asks me what Americans think of Palestinians, and I try to answer, throwing in that the killing of collaborators hasn't gone over

J. SACCO 1·94

too well, from mid '90 to mid '91 83 alleged collaborators were killed in Gaza by other Palestinians, which is more than two and a half times those killed here by Israeli security forces in the same period... And Ibrahim says he doesn't care about American public opinion, he says, "We can't have these collaborators among us, assassinating us, telling

the Israelis what they know," and someone else says before the intifada the collaborators did as they pleased, now they're paying, he says maybe ten have been killed in Nuseirat, and someone recalls one collaborator being shoved down a street, the people beating him with their shoes, then a couple of cars drove

up with members of the Unified Leadership and Hamas, they took him to an orange grove and killed him. And they say sometimes the suspect's confession is taped and then played in cassette shops for everyone to hear, and, yes, they admit some suspects may be tortured, but Ibrahim says, "We have no jails, no imprisonment. There is no other way to deal with these people."

J. SACCO 1-94

Our party breaks up, the neighbors need to get home before the 8 o'clock curfew...

the rest of us cross the sandy area to a new room...

We settle in... Ibrahim tends to the coals while the rain beats hard on the corrugated asbestos roof...

This is the room of Ibrahim's brother...

Ibrahim's brother has been pretty quiet most of the evening...

I've been told his name two or three times... what was it?... Ammar

Ammar's wife and children have been sent elsewhere to make room for us...

Ibrahim's family lives in the other part of the house, the part with the new couch...

And by the way Ibrahim is telling us about Abu Jihad, how the PLO fighters held off the Israelis in Beirut — and with the jets dropping their phosphorous bombs!

Every time a topic dries up and we pass some moments in silence, Ammar welcomes us again in the Arab fashion...

AHLAN WA SAHLAN.

And we respond:

AHLAN BEEK.

After Ibrahim leaves to be with his family, Ammar fetches some papers...

...a medical report written by a Palestinian doctor, it begins "To Whom It May Concern"...

The subject is a 28-year-old woman from Nuseirat camp with "severe dyspnea, cyanosis and chest infections," she has "bronchiectasis bilateral advanced corpulmonale and episodes of C.H.F.," she needs a transplant of heart and lungs. A Montreal doctor has offered to do the lungs gratis, but there are other costs..."immune suppressive medications, physiotherapy, rehabilitation," and—

J. SACCO 1·94

Ammar wants to know if I can get the report to someone in the West... if I can find another doctor or hospital that would help her... if there's something I can do...

I DON'T—
I—
TELL HIM I'LL TRY TO TAKE THIS TO A DOCTOR.

Now Ammar and Larry are talking amongst themselves in Arabic... and then...

HE SAYS HE HASN'T WORKED IN TWO YEARS.

HE TRIED TO START A BUSINESS REPAIRING REFRIGERATORS BUT IT NEVER GOT OFF THE GROUND.

HE SAYS THERE'S NO WORK IN GAZA...

HE SAYS THE ISRAELIS ISSUE FEW PERMITS TO WORK IN ISRAEL...

HE SAYS IT'S NOT POSSIBLE FOR PALESTINIANS TO WORK IN THE GULF STATES SINCE THE WAR...

HE WANTS TO KNOW IF IT'S POSSIBLE FOR HIM TO GET WORK IN THE WEST...

HE'S ASKING ME?
I—
YOU KNOW I THINK IT'S PRETTY HARD TO ARRANGE WORK IN THE U.S. ... EUROPE I'M NOT SO SURE ABOUT BUT I THINK IT'D BE HARD THERE, TOO...
I DON'T KNOW...

Larry tells him...

AHLAN WA SAHLAN.

AHLAN BEEK.

J. SACCO 1·94

In the morning, Ammar is a little more upbeat...

He's got ideas...

Maybe he can go into business with Ibrahim and Masud...

Ibrahim and Masud make desks and fixtures on the side...

Yeah, then maybe the three of them can get a loan from Save the Children...

I suggest an UNRWA fund I've heard about...

I don't really know what I'm talking about, but I'm set on keeping things bright and cheerful...

After breakfast, we walk to Block 1...

It rained again last night...

LAW

Now we're in another room, sitting around with another group of men...

The fellow behind the desk is a lawyer, he handles military and civil cases...

WHAT ARE YOU WORKING ON NOW? WHAT'S THAT FILE ON YOUR DESK?

A CASE OF FAMILY HONOR...

A 15-YEAR-OLD GIRL KILLED BY HER FAMILY... I'M DEFENDING THE KILLER, THE WITNESSES, THOSE WHO BROUGHT THE ROPE...

SHE WAS MARRIED, SHE COMMITTED ADULTERY WITH A COLLABORATOR...

HER FAMILY STRANGLED HER.

Islamic law, he says, calls for death to adulterers...

The same punishment would have been meted out to the collaborator, he says, but he's under Israeli protection...

Typically, he says, adulterers are shunned, treated as pariahs... he says killings like this one are unusual... in this case, he says, the family took the law into its own hands...

THE ISRAELIS WANT TO HANDLE THIS CASE IN A MILITARY COURT BECAUSE THEIR COLLABORATOR IS INVOLVED...

MY CASE RESTS ON THE FOURTH GENEVA CONVENTION, WHICH REQUIRES AN OCCUPYING POWER TO RESPECT THE LAWS AND MORES OF THE TERRITORY IT OCCUPIES...

ALSO, THE JEWISH AND CHRISTIAN TRADITIONS CALL FOR THE SAME PUNISHMENT FOR ADULTERY*

THIS IS A RELIGIO[US] CASE AND SHOULD N[OT] SIT BEFOR[E] A MILITARY COURT.

*SEE DEUTERONOMY 22:22-27, FOR EX.

J. SACCO 3·94

160

BLACK COFFEE

SONS OF THE CURFEW

In the Gaza Strip, nighttime is curfew time...

750,000 Palestinians cannot leave their homes from 8 p.m. to 4 a.m.....

Those've been Israeli orders for upwards of three and a half years...*

So we're inside again...

Ammar's room...

MY SON WAS BORN IN THE MORNING, IN THE EVENING MY WIFE CAME HOME WITH HIM, AND IN THE NIGHT THEY PUT A TOTAL CURFEW ON US, ONE OF THE LONGEST...

THAT IS WHY WE NICKNAMED HIM "FATHER OF THE CURFEW."

WE PALESTINIANS, WE LIKE CHILDREN, WE LIKE BIG FAMILIES, IT IS VERY GOOD. BUT YOU DON'T LIKE BIG FAMILIES IN THE WEST?

IN THE WEST, SOME PEOPLE FEEL IT'S NOT A GOOD WORLD TO BRING CHILDREN INTO.

*AS OF FEB. 1992

J. SACCO 2.94

It's not a good world, and these refugees' sons of a refugee's sons are growing up knowing the score...

They've been taught to distinguish between where they're *from*—a village disappeared by the Zionists in 1948—and where they *live*—Nuseirat camp, Block 2...

After the children are put to sleep, Ibrahim leafs through my guidebook. He stops at an illustration of an Arab and a donkey...

IT IS AN ISRAELI BOOK?

NO, I THINK IT'S AUSTRALIAN.

IS THIS HOW THEY THINK OF US? LEADING A DONKEY?

YOU WILL TELL THEM WHAT YOU SEE HERE!

IN MY FAMILY, MY COUSINS, WE HAVE STUDENTS! A PROFESSOR! A TEACHER OF COMPUTERS!

ARABS HAVE TECHNOLOGY! AND WE PALESTINIANS *LOVE* EDUCATION!

YOU SHOULD DRAW SHAMIR'S FACE ON THE ARAB AND BEGIN'S ON THE DONKEY!*

Later, a dog is barking... Ibrahim turns down the Oum Koulsoum cassette...

Vehicles are passing outside...

THE SOLDIERS.

Israel a travel survival kit Neil Tilbury

*MENACHEM BEGIN- former prime minister of Israel. YITZHAK SHAMIR—then current prime minister.

167

TOMATOES

In the morning, we visit the workshop where Ibrahim and Masud make the desks...

Masud explains the set-up, how the operation works...

Ammar would like to work here, too...

I want to take a photo, I tell them to pretend they're working on a desk...

Ammar pretends he's putting in a screw...

The make-believe is over, it's time to head out...

J. SACCO 3.94

I'm supposed to meet someone in Deir el-Balah, that guy at the lawyer's with all those questions...just to show there weren't any hard feelings, he invited me to tour the family greenhouses...

Ammar knows his house...

Here we are...nice place...

On the way, the cousin rails against Israel's stranglehold on the Palestinian agricultural sector...

And he ain't joshing, just take the for instance of getting goods to market...

introductions...

a cousin once removed...

we'll go in his car...

Trucking produce a few dozen miles from Gaza to the West Bank requires six different permits...

the vehicle pass alone needs clearance from five different offices...

the produce permit requires a 12,000 shekel advance to the Value Added Tax Authorities (and, incidentally, while Israeli farmers can expect refunds on the 18 percent VAT on inputs, Palestinian farmers get no such break)...

Given those hurdles and the necessity of going through Israeli middlemen, a Gazan farmer shipping to Europe typically pays twice the air freight as his Israeli counterpart...

170

Perhaps the sorest point is Israel's dominance of Palestinian water resources... the Israelis pump West Bank water to Israel and Jewish settlements at such a rate that only 17 percent is left for Palestinians... Here in Gaza, Israel controls 35 percent of the water supply, and the drilling of 200-meter wells from the settlements has increased the salinity in shallow Palestinian wells to dangerous levels... It can be not just unhealthy to drink —the salty water damages Gazan crops...

Meanwhile, the Israelis all but forbid Gazans to dig new wells or deepen existing ones...

Despite all this, these guys want to prove that Palestinians know how to grow a tomato...

See them?

See how good they are?

Here, take some!

take!

J. SACCO 3-94

While we're out here, they inspect the damage from last night's storm. On the way over we've seen dozens of greenhouses ripped open. Some of theirs are damaged, too, and each greenhouse costs $5,000, they say...

ONE SHEKEL TO GAZA TOWN

Chapter Seven

Sameh paid his, sort of...

He'd let his electric meter run the first ten days of the month till it racked up about $50 worth. Then he'd stop it...

What could he do? He hadn't earned any money in two years...

He lived off savings he'd made working abroad and off his father's slim wage as a day laborer in Israel...

Sameh was anything but idle, however; he did volunteer social work at the camp's rehabilitation center, a facility he and several others had helped set up...

He told me the story once, how he and the others made proposals, enlisted the support of community leaders and health organizations, how they'd gone door-to-door for funds...

Now the facility had a staff of volunteer teachers, its own syllabus, and two dozen deaf and dumb students...

By Jabalia standards it was a roaring success...

J. SACCO 5·94

182

People were spreading plastic sheets over their roofs to stop the leaking, hoping bags of stones would hold the plastic down in the wind...

In one house, an old man demonstrated the water damage by picking chunks from a wall with his hands...

HE'S ASKING US TO STAY FOR TEA.

LET'S MOVE ON.

One woman showed us a room where a section of roof had blown off in the storm. Plastic was covering the hole...

SHE SAYS IT COSTS $200 TO REPLACE THE ROOF...

THEY'VE GONE TO THE UNITED NATIONS DEVELOPMENT PROGRAM FOR HELP, BUT THERE WERE MANY PEOPLE THERE WITH THE SAME PROBLEM... THEY WERE TURNED AWAY.

I asked if I could take a photo...she misunderstood, thought I wanted her picture...

NO, I WANT A PICTURE OF THE DAMAGE...

Maybe I should've taken her picture after all...

J. SACCO 4.94

Sameh's two sisters, for example, lived with their husbands and kids and three other families in a single dwelling, 10 meters by 10 meters— 35 people all together, seven to a room...

THE CHILDREN.

For such a crowded camp, there were some large empty spaces...

In 1971, in order to facilitate the pacification of Gaza, General Ariel Sharon's bulldozers cut swaths through this and other refugee camps— widening roads, isolating sections, giving IDF vehicles more room to maneuver...

Back then the Israelis bulldozed 40 houses a day in Jabalia, you can still see traces of the foundations where homes had been...

186

After the days' excursions, after curfew, when the rains and wind seemed to be at their strongest and you could practically hear the camp getting damaged, Sameh and I would sit in his rooms and tell each other the stories of our lives...

He had studied in Cairo and taught philosophy in Yemen...

Except for the space between the walls and the roof and the rain leaking in, Sameh lived about as comfortably as any Palestinian refugee I'd ever met...

He had a lot of space to himself...

he had chairs, a dining room table, other furniture...

a Western-style toilet...

indoor plants...

paintings and prints on the walls, abstracts, impressionism...

He'd created as much of a refuge for himself as circumstances allowed...

Sameh made me feel comfortable in his place, so much so that initially I felt uncomfortable...

YOU WILL SLEEP IN THE BED, I WILL SLEEP ON THE FLOOR...

IT'S COLD ON THE FLOOR, AND THIS IS YOUR BED. I'LL SLEEP ON THE FLOOR...

but I always got the bed, the only warm place in the house...

J. SACCO 5·94

187

And this is where the uprising began — Jabalia refugee camp...

...it was a spontaneous, popular explosion, and it caught everyone by surprise, including the PLO...

until then, most Palestinian resistance had generated from outside of historical Palestine...

but on that December day in 1987, Palestinians living under Israeli occupation for more than 20 years took things into their own hands...

Mohammed and Husein lead us between refugee homes and the outer fence of the IDF base, a three- or four-meter passage...

We come to a long, muddy road, it's that way to the cemetery...

That's where the Palestinian workers are buried...

They were returning from their jobs in Israel... There was a collision with an Israeli vehicle ...Some say the Israeli driver did it intentionally...

Four Palestinians died...

Anyway, the dead are buried up the road...

There's wash on the barbed wire, women can step out of their front doors to hang it...

It's too cold, we decide not to visit the graves...

191

THE BOYS

PART THREE

Firas is 15 years old and works for the Popular Front for the Liberation of Palestine, one of the resistance groups that began influencing the uprising within weeks of the initial unrest...

WHY ARE YOU INVOLVED IN THE INTIFADA?

FOR ME IT IS A WAY OF TAKING BACK MY COUNTRY, TO BE FREE OF THE OCCUPATION, TO LET THE PEOPLE OF THE WORLD KNOW ABOUT US...

I SEE HOW THE SOLDIERS TREAT MY PARENTS. THEY BEAT MY BROTHERS. ONE OF MY BROTHERS IS IN JAIL...

HOW WERE YOU RECRUITED BY THE POPULAR FRONT?

"My neighbor came to me... He asked about my politics, whether I agreed with the policies of Hamas or the other groups. He left me for a couple of days. He was examining me, seeing who my friends are, where I'd go...

"When he decided I might be the right man, he asked whether I wanted to work with the Popular Front. He said I should consider it if I cared about myself and my country, about our problems here and the life we live. I said I'd think about it. He didn't force me. I sat with him and some others six times before deciding. Other groups approached me, but I'd already decided on the Popular Front..."

HOW OLD WERE YOU WHEN YOU DECIDED?

I WAS 13.

"Five soldiers took me from my bed and threw me to the ground... The fall broke my arm...

When they saw me clutching my arm, they started kicking it... Doctors and nurses tried to stop

them, but they were pushed away... The soldiers broke the arm of a hospital employee, too...

I couldn't count how many times I was beaten... Blood was coming from my mouth

and nose... They broke a tooth..."

AFTER TWO DAYS I REGAINED CONSCIOUSNESS...

THE SOLDIERS CAME AGAIN, BUT SOME U.N. AND RED CROSS PEOPLE WERE THERE, AND THEY COULDN'T BEAT ME.

The interview concluded, Sameh and I sit around discussing Firas and kids his age...

OUR LEADERSHIP HAS KEPT THE YOUTH CLUBS CLOSED. THE KIDS DON'T PLAY FOOTBALL, AND THEIR OTHER INTERESTS ARE CUT OFF...

ALL THEY'RE SUPPOSED TO THINK ABOUT IS THE STRUGGLE. THEY SING SONGS ABOUT THE INTIFADA, EVEN IN SCHOOL...

ALSO, THE SOLDIERS WON'T LET ANYONE ALONE. THEY'RE ALWAYS STOPPING YOU, ASKING YOU QUESTIONS...AND EVERY HOME HERE HAS SOMEONE WHO IS IMPRISONED, WHO HAS DIED, WHO IS WOUNDED...

THIS IS THE CHILDHOOD?

J. SACCO 7.94

I'm listening to him, thinking back to an interview I had a couple of weeks back with the head of the YMCA Rehabilitation Programme in East Jerusalem...

His organization works with young, wounded Palestinians...

WHAT ARE WE GOING TO DO WITH THE GREAT NUMBER OF INJURED? IF WE GET A STATE, HOW WILL WE DEAL WITH THEM?

DO WE COMPENSATE THEM FOR WOUNDS THEY RECEIVED IN THE INTIFADA?

One of his chief concerns is integrating seriously injured youths back into the community...

THERE'S ONE GIRL, SHE'S 14 YEARS OLD, A BULLET PUT OUT HER EYE...

FOR TEN DAYS AFTERWARDS SHE DIDN'T TALK TO ANYONE...

HER MOTHER WAS WORRIED THAT THE DISFIGUREMENT WOULD END THE GIRL'S PROSPECTS FOR MARRIAGE...

WE HAD TO VISIT THE MOTHER TO CALM HER, SO SHE WOULDN'T MAKE HER DAUGHTER LOSE HEART...

Sameh and I are at the rehab center, in the middle of tea and a chat, when a woman walks in with her kid...

the child is mentally retarded...

the woman wants to find him a school... is there room for him in the deaf class?

Sameh explains it'd do the boy no good to be in with deaf kids...

the mother and child leave...

HANDICAPPED

The fact is, Sameh tells me, only five people in Gaza work in the field of special education, and none have specialized training...Here in Jabalia, he says, there are 1200 handicapped people, and little money to do anything for them...

The rehabilitation center tries to provide lunch and help with clothes for the deaf students...

"But there's no real budget," says Sameh. "It's hard to plan. The country is poor...

and hearing aids cost hundreds of dollars each...

The center doesn't have the resources, but there's no end of ideas to help the kids...

WE ARE COORDINATING WITH UNRWA TO ACCEPT THE CLEVER ONES IN THE NORMAL SCHOOLS. THEY'VE AGREED TO DO THIS...

FOR THOSE WITHOUT THE ABILITY, WE WANT TO START A VOCATIONAL PROGRAM... WE WANT TO ARRANGE WORK WITH EMPLOYERS IN THE COMMUNITY...

ALSO, WE HAVE TO EDUCATE THE COMMUNITY ABOUT THE HANDICAPPED. WE HAVE TO CHANGE THEIR ATTITUDES. A GOOD WAY IS TO SHOW BY EXAMPLE: HERE IS A HANDICAPPED PERSON, SEE WHAT HE CAN DO...

J. SACCO 7-94

Sameh talks of developing a professional program here, but I've been told that certain of the center's directors owe their positions <u>not</u> to professional qualifications, but to factional loyalties...Fateh, this source said, got involved only <u>after</u> the center had already established itself and now enjoys the PR windfall of association with a successful program while providing little in promised material support...

In addition to those problems, Sameh admits that neither he nor the teachers are professionally trained to work with the handicapped... he <u>wants</u> training... in fact, UNRWA had just nominated him to Bethlehem University for a four-month course that seems right up his alley—Developing Skills for Those Working with Persons with Disabilities...

but Bethlehem is in the West Bank and Sameh lives in Gaza, and travelling back and forth requires Israeli permission...

THEY SAID NO? WHY?

BECAUSE IT'S NOT A PROGRAM AFFILIATED WITH UNRWA...

Still, Sameh dreams about furthering his education...

I'D LIKE TO GO FOR A MASTER'S DEGREE ... I WANT TO STUDY IN EUROPE, WHERE THEY HAVE A HUMANE UNDERSTANDING OF THE HANDI-CAPPED...

I WANT TO GET ANOTHER NATIONALITY SO I CAN TRAVEL ABROAD FREELY AND COME AND WORK IN PALES-TINE WITH NO PROBLEM...

But it's the Israelis who'll decide whether Sameh can travel or not... and, in any case, the center doesn't have the money to send someone abroad for two or three years...

Hell, the center can't even afford a wage for him or its six teachers... they get nothing for full-time work...

Meanwhile, the $5,000 Sameh saved while teaching in Yemen is about to run out...

then what?

I'm blinking fast, snapping mental pictures and thinking, "This'll make a great couple of pages in the comic" —a weird scene of a pitching car with the rain going torrential while Sameh strains to see over his shoulder into the dark and fumbles with the gears to back us out of another washed-out path... and that's me next to him and this is my happiest moment... I've made it, you understand, I've come hundreds of miles via planes and buses and taxis to be precisely here: <u>Jabalia</u>, the must-see refugee camp of the Gaza Strip, the intifada's ground zero, a Disneyland of refuse and squalor... and here I am, brushing up against the Palestinian experience, a goddamn adventure cartoonist who hasn't changed his clothes in days, who's stepped over a few dead rats and shivered from the cold, who's bullshitted with the boys and nodded knowingly at their horrible narratives... and I'm pinching myself in a car in the dark in a flood, giddy from the ferocity outside, thinking, "Throw it at me, baby, I can take it," but I've got the window rolled up tight...

Amateur footage... battles with soldiers... wounded youths, blood, gore...

IN THE FIRST WEEKS OF THE INTIFADA, I ALMOST QUIT BECAUSE OF THAT KIND OF THING...

[He's a nurse.]

Next, the infamous CBS spot of soldiers beating a couple of kids they'd just arrested, methodically breaking their arms. I've read about this, but never seen it...it goes on a little too long...

After some rah-rah Palestine stuff — film of PLO guerrillas training and some MTV-style anthems — we get to a home video... a burial of a youth... he's just been shot dead in a clash ... the mourners are quick... tense... they're on the lookout ... Some Palestinians are convinced the Israelis use the bodies of the fallen shebab as a source of human organs... it's jerky footage... hand-held...they're tense, have I said that? watching out for soldiers, afraid soldiers will come...

that's that, now we're sitting around, talking...

I've got my eye on the clock...

It's getting close to eight o'clock, the curfew...

maybe no one else has noticed...

maybe the clock is fast...

maybe I should say something...

211

Early the next morning, Sameh heads off to the center. I usually go with him, but not today. I tell him I want to sleep in, I tell him I want to catch up on my journal...

Later, Sameh's brother and his pal stop by to see if I want to watch the video again. I can count my Arabic on my fingers and toes, I can't explain I'd rather not...

We watch the video over lunch, tea, and sweets...

...the wounds and blood, the arm-snapping, they're easier to stomach the second time around...

at the burial, the mourners are still tense and on the lookout, but I'm not going to worry, I've seen this before, the soldiers won't come...

that's the good thing about video, you can re-wind it, watch it over, elim-inate all surprises... it's easier on your nerves, you can sip tea, you've seen it before, you know the sol-diers won't come... guaranteed.

step out-side, how-ever, in present time, and all bets are off...

J. SACCO 8·94

Chapter Eight

PILGRIMAGE

He knows why I'm here, he knows my time is limited, I want real stories, he knows that, vivid descriptions, the details, man, comics is a visual medium...

How many soldiers? How did they beat you? Then what happened? He helps me wring it out of the people I interview...

And he's heard every blow and humiliation described twice, once by the person telling me, and again when it's come out of his mouth in translation...

That'd make a good picture...

We have an evening to kill and we spend it with Sameh's family—his ill mother, his brother and sister-in-law, a nephew, a niece, an unmarried sister...

His mother talks a little about 1948, but her sentences trail off, tears well up...

THEY THREW US OUT OF OUR HOMES, AND NOW THEY'VE FOLLOWED US HERE...

His nephew is 15 years old and has been shot twice in clashes. But we're tired of talking about clashes...

Sameh's brother is curious...

I WONDER HOW YOU'VE COME TO EAT AND SLEEP HERE. AREN'T YOU AFRAID AFTER ALL YOU'VE HEARD ABOUT US?

The niece is staring at me. She's 10 years old and fascinated. Sameh translates...

WHAT DOES THE WATER TASTE LIKE IN YOUR COUNTRY?

IS IT BETTER WATER HERE OR THERE?

DO YOU HAVE THE SOLDIERS AND THE JEWS AND FATEH AND THE POPULAR FRONT IN YOUR COUNTRY?

DO THE WOMEN WEAR PANTS OUTSIDE LIKE THEY DO IN EGYPT?

CAN A MAN HAVE TWO WIVES?

229

To get to the shops on the other side of the street, we hop from one pile of refuse to another...

Sameh doesn't find anything he likes...

It's time to go to Rafah...

J. SACCO 12-94

A short car ride later and we're sitting in a home in a refugee camp with a woman and her youngest son... Tea is served, I get my pen out, and we get right to business... Sameh is translating...

WE WERE SITTING HERE WHEN THE SOLDIERS ATTACKED OUR AREA...

"They were throwing gas... so the children and old people became sick...

"A gas bomb landed in our courtyard...

"The women went out, shouting for help. All the people were running out, gathering... throwing stones at the soldiers...

"The youth put up a barricade, including a fridge. They didn't want the jeeps to enter...

"I told my neighbors, 'Why are you staying in your house? The soldiers might be coming to take our sons... We have to stop them...'

"My son Basel wanted to help the people affected by the tear gas. He went to see if the soldiers were still outside...

235

"I got up and went to the market to get some rice for the wake of my uncle's son...

"...People there looked at me strangely. They knew Ahmed had just been shot, but they didn't want to tell me...

"I entered my house but no one was there...

"A neighbor told me four students had been injured in a clash at the school... Two of my sons went to that school...

"I went to my daughter-in-law. She didn't want to tell me anything, and then she started crying. She said, 'Ahmed is injured.'

"We went to the hospital in Khan Younis, but we didn't find him there...

"They told us the soldiers had taken him to an army hospital in Israel. I couldn't control myself. I thought the same thing would happen that happened to my son Basel...

"We left to see him. It took us till 6 p.m. ...

"He had been shot five times... in the forehead, the neck, the arm, the heart, and the cheek. He was still alive...

"We wanted to take him to Al-Makassad hospital in Jerusalem... but they refused...

239

"I asked again the next day. I went to the director to kiss his feet and hands to let me take my son...

"He told me I had to bring Arab doctors and an ambulance to take him...

"My son, Ahmed's brother, went back to Gaza to get the ambulance and doctors, and they returned when it was dark...

"When the Arab doctors saw him, they advised us not to take him. They knew he would be dead soon, but they told us it was because the road was bad.

"That night...we left for Gaza. We left two people at the hospital... They slept there...

"At 1 a.m. the soldiers woke them to tell them Ahmed had died. They said they would bring them the body...

"But they took them and left them on a road in Israel in the middle of the night...

"They walked 10 kilometers before they reached a petrol station... and they had to wait till 4 a.m. to cross into Gaza because of the night curfew...

"In Rafah we hadn't received a phone call. The soldiers put a curfew on the town... so how was I going to go to the hospital to see my son?

"The two who had been with Ahmed reached the camp. They told my son, Ahmed's brother...

"My son didn't want to tell me directly. He said, 'If he's dead, he's better off than us.' 'No!' I said, and I knew Ahmed was dead...

"My son and husband went to the military to get Ahmed's body. The soldiers said they would bring him at eight o'clock...

"We wanted to bury him next to his brother, but the soldiers refused... until we phoned a human rights organization in Jerusalem. They intervened on our behalf...

THE EGYPTIAN BORDER?

YES.

I know, everyone's exhausted, but we're almost done, and then I'll check Rafah off my list...

At the frontier, a woman is yelling across the barbed wire and fences of no-man's-land to someone in Egypt...

WHAT'S SHE SAY?

HOW ARE YOU DOING OVER THERE? SAY HELLO TO SO-AND-SO...

Sadat went to Jerusalem in '77, Nobel Prizes for Peace were divvied up, and Egypt and Israel concluded a separate peace. Egypt got back the Sinai, captured by Israel in '67, and the two parties settled on their border, which was bulldozed right through Rafah, a Palestinian town. Most of Rafah's inhabitants live on this side, but a few thousand are stranded in Egypt...

Two women are sitting on rocks waiting for a friend or relative on the Egyptian side to show up...

We leave them to their waiting...

Yousef drives us to the taxis. It's time to get back to Gaza Town...

HE SAYS IF YOU REALLY WANT TO SEE RAFAH, YOU NEED AT LEAST A WEEK.

YES. I'M SORRY I DON'T HAVE MORE TIME.

Near Gaza Town, the roads are washed out. We have to approach from another direction...

WELCOME TO GAZA עזה

Chapter Nine

And standing there with two girls from Tel Aviv, it occurs to me that I *have* seen the Israelis, but through Palestinian eyes—that Israelis were mainly soldiers and settlers to me now, too...

I guide them through the Jewish Quarter to the Western Wall...

We talk some more and I drop my guard, I tell them about my project, that I've come to meet Palestinians...

YOU'VE BEEN HERE TWO MONTHS AND YOU HAVEN'T BEEN TO TEL AVIV?

TO HAIFA?

SHOULDN'T YOU BE SEEING *OUR* SIDE OF THE STORY, TOO?

And what can I say? I say I've heard nothing but the Israeli side most all my life, that it'd take a whole other trip to see Israel, that I'd like to meet Israelis, but that wasn't why I was here...

DO YOU WANT TO WALK THROUGH THE ARAB MARKET?

NO NO! IT'S TOO DANGEROUS!

NOTHING WILL HAPPEN. IT'S REALLY COLORFUL, THERE'S ALL THESE STALLS AND SHOPS. NOTHING'S EVER HAPPENED TO ME.

JEWS GET STABBED IN THERE.

I SEE ORTHODOX JEWS WALKING THROUGH THERE... AND THERE'S ALWAYS TOURISTS.

I'LL GO.

WELL, I'M NOT GOING.

And I couldn't find the people I wanted... the young girl with the gunshot wound I'd come to visit was no longer at the hospital...

And at the nearby Balata refugee camp, my pal Jabril wasn't home either...

I'd come to say my goodbyes ...I'm leaving...in less than a week I'll be back in Cairo, and then on to Berlin...

Yeah, Berlin...

but, meanwhile, it's pleasant enough to be in Tel Aviv, which seems familiar, somehow, to my Western ears and eyes...

Naomi and Paula seem familiar, too... their day-to-day concerns remind me of the stuff that makes up the lives of people I know in Europe, the States...

261

J. SACCO 6·95

But these women are from Israel, let there be no doubt, and so what if Paula's roots are Eastern European and Naomi's grandparents came from Germany? Germany!!

And both can look back to ancestors who helped make a home for the Jews right here... Naomi says her relatives were well known Zionists, and Paula says her granddad was a Pioneer...

I NEVER WANT TO GO THERE! THIS IS MY HOME!

And what they want to do now is live ordinary lives here, to live in peace. Yes, peace, and I'm almost sorry to bring it up, but let's get specific, and over lunch we do, and both admit they go back and forth on the particulars...

Naomi, for example, is concerned with security considerations...

WHAT SECURITY CONSIDERATIONS DO YOU MEAN?

HAVE YOU LOOKED AT A MAP? HAVE YOU SEEN HOW SMALL ISRAEL IS?

THE WAY THINGS ARE NOW, WE HAVE OUR HILLS, THE JORDANIANS HAVE THEIR HILLS, AND THE RIVER JORDAN RUNS DOWN THE MIDDLE...

IF WE GIVE UP THE WEST BANK, THE ARABS WILL HAVE ALL THE HILLS, AND THEY'LL OVERLOOK ISRAEL...

Hills! The high ground! Ask anyone with a mind for combat, the high ground confers the greatest advantage...

BUT THEN THERE WERE THE IRAQI MISSILES IN THE GULF WAR...

SOME PEOPLE SAY THE MISSILES SHOWED ISRAEL IS VULNERABLE WITH OR WITHOUT THE HILLS...

But they've got other misgivings about what peace might bring, namely—

CAN WE TRUST THE ARABS?

WE CAN MAKE PEACE WITH THEM NOW, OKAY, BUT WHO'S TO SAY THEY WON'T GET SOME LEADER IN THE FUTURE WHO WANTS TO DESTROY ISRAEL— LIKE NASSAR*?

*GAMAL ABD-AL NASSAR—Egyptian leader of 1950's and 60's who promoted and symbolized Arab nationalism and unity.

J. SACCO 6-95

262

THE ARABS GO CRAZY. THEY'VE STARTED OTHER WARS.

LOOK AT SADAT. HE CAME TO JERUSALEM, HE WANTED PEACE, LOOK WHAT HAPPENED TO HIM.

I UNDERSTAND, BUT YOU HAVE EXTREMISTS IN ISRAEL, TOO.

SURE WE HAVE EXTREMISTS, BUT YOU DIDN'T SEE ANYONE HERE SHOOTING MENACHEM BEGIN FOR SIGNING A PEACE TREATY WITH EGYPT...

OKAY, BUT FROM A PALESTINIAN PERSPECTIVE, ISRAEL'S EXPANSION OF THE SETTLEMENTS DOESN'T EXACTLY BUILD TRUST EITHER.

I'M AGAINST THE SETTLEMENTS!

AND WHAT ABOUT JERUSALEM? THE ISRAELI GOVERNMENT REFUSES TO EVEN CONSIDER GIVING THE OCCUPIED PART UP...

NO, WE CAN NEVER GIVE UP JERUSALEM. THE CITY CANNOT BE DIVIDED AGAIN.

IT'S THE SYMBOL OF ISRAEL.

JERUSALEM REPRESENTS WHAT'S OLD AND WHAT'S NEW ABOUT JEWISH HERITAGE. THE TEMPLE WAS THERE.

ARE YOU RELIGIOUS?

NO, BUT THERE'S SOMETHING ABOUT JERUSALEM, I'M NOT SURE WHAT. WE HAVE SO MUCH HISTORY THERE. JERUSALEM IS WHY JEWS RETURNED TO THIS PART OF THE WORLD...

I MEAN, COULD YOU IMAGINE A JEWISH HOMELAND IN UGANDA?

WELL, WHAT ABOUT A PALESTINIAN STATE? CAN YOU IMAGINE THAT?

I DON'T KNOW. MAYBE. BUT COULD IT BE ECONOMICALLY VIABLE? I KNOW THINGS IN THE REFUGEE CAMPS ARE BAD, BUT IN GENERAL CONDITIONS ARE BETTER FOR THE ARABS UNDER OCCUPATION THAN THEY WERE BEFORE.

I THINK THAT'S SORT OF A MYTH. THE TERRITORIES ARE ECONOMICALLY SUPPRESSED. THEY'RE A CAPTIVE MARKET AND A SOURCE OF CHEAP LABOR FOR ISRAEL...

AND AS FAR AS ECONOMIC VIABILITY IS CONCERNED, SHOULD THAT BE A CONDITION FOR STATEHOOD? WHERE WOULD ISRAEL BE WITHOUT THE MONEY IT GETS FROM THE STATES?

I DON'T LIKE OUR DEPENDENCE ON THE U.S. FOR MONEY.

J. SACCO 6·95

BUT ASIDE FROM ALL THAT, THE PALESTINIANS WANT TO RULE THEMSELVES. THE OCCUPATION IS HARSH. DO YOU REALLY KNOW WHAT GOES ON OVER THERE?

ISRAELIS ARE TIRED OF APOLOGIZING FOR THE OCCUPIED TERRITORIES! THERE WAS A WAR! WE WON THE LAND IN THE WAR! IT'S *OUR* LAND NOW!

I'M NOT TRYING TO PROVOKE YOU, I'M—

PERHAPS I DON'T KNOW EVERYTHING THAT'S GOING ON, BUT MY BROTHER SERVED THERE, AND AFTERWARDS HE HAD TO SEE A PSYCHOLOGIST.

I KNOW A GUY WHO SERVED IN GAZA AND HIS NOSE WAS CRUSHED BY A STONE.

Yikes! But when we met in Jerusalem, she said—

I'M SORRY ABOUT WHAT HAPPENS TO PALESTINIANS, BUT THE SOLDIERS DON'T SHOOT ANYONE WITHOUT A WARNING...

FIRST THEY FIRE INTO THE AIR AND THEN AT THE LEGS, AND ANYONE WHO KILLS SOMEONE WITHOUT FOLLOWING REGULATIONS GOES ON TRIAL AND GETS SENT TO PRISON. I KNOW OF A CASE RIGHT NOW.

WELL, FROM TALKING TO PALESTINIANS WHO'VE BEEN SHOT, IT SOUNDS A LOT LESS DISCRIMINATING THAN THAT.

I'M NOT SAYING THERE'S NOT A MORAL PROBLEM WITH THE OCCUPATION...

BUT WHAT ABOUT PALESTINIANS WHO KILL PALESTINIANS THEY ACCUSE OF COLLABORATING WITH ISRAEL?

WHAT ABOUT PALESTINIAN TERRORISM?

WHAT ABOUT BURNING ISRAELI CHILDREN TO DEATH IN A CAR IN GAZA?

WELL, I'M NOT GOING TO DEFEND *THAT*...

BUT IS IT ALL TERRORISM TO YOU? WHAT ABOUT WHEN PALESTINIANS TAKE MILITARY ACTION AGAINST THE OCCUPATION FORCES?

DO THEY HAVE THAT RIGHT AT ALL?

WE JUST WANT TO LIVE OUR LIVES, OKAY? WE HAVE *OUR LIVES*! WE HAVE JOBS AND FAMILIES AND WE GO OUT AND LIVE JUST LIKE *YOU* DO... WE DON'T THINK ABOUT THIS STUFF ALL THE TIME, AND WE GET A BIT TIRED OF HEARING ABOUT IT!

IT'S NOT THAT WE'RE TIRED...

BUT WHEN YOU HEAR IT OVER AND OVER, YOU GET...

TIRED...

J. SACCO 695

more tear gas!

the tear gas goes up...

and comes down on the roofs of the old city...

let's hope not through someone's kitchen window...

And I look over to Jabril and he's already a couple dozen paces away...

I've got my camera out, and he won't exactly endear himself to the IDF if they come over and find him with me...

After the commotion, our lucky reunion doesn't seem as sweet. We leave each other a few minutes later...

J. SACCO 6.95

NABLUS

Nablus, back in Nablus... and here the taxi drivers tell me, as far as they know, it's possible to get to Jenin and back... I have an hour or so to kill...

Things are busy in Nablus... The morning's shopping is in full swing...

A couple of vendors call me over, pour me coffee...

The guy selling orange juice salutes me playfully as I walk by...

J. SACCO 6.95

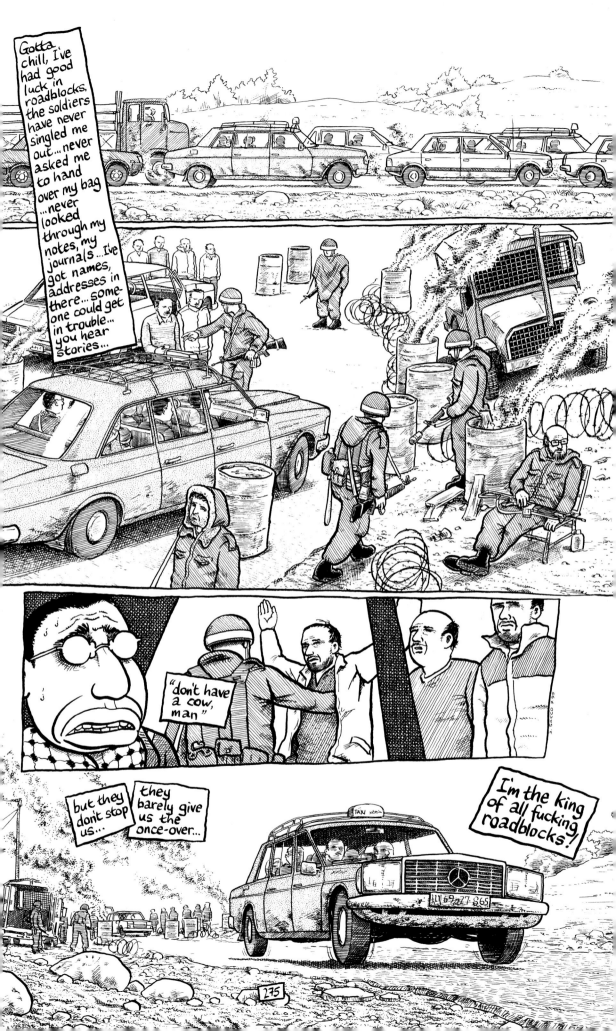

Gotta chill, I've had good luck in roadblocks, the soldiers have never singled me out... never asked me to hand over my bag ...never looked through my notes, my journals...I've got names, addresses in there...some-one could get in trouble... you hear stories...

"don't have a cow, man"

but they don't stop us...

they barely give us the once-over...

I'm the king of all fucking roadblocks!

JENIN

All right, I got here late, I've missed my appointment, so I wander aimlessly until I come across an older man, an ex-school teacher... he sits under the gaze of Israeli soldiers in their rooftop positions and gets to speculating about the future of Palestine and the Palestinians...

'TO BE OR NOT TO BE... THAT IS THE QUESTION.'

'HAMLET'

YES. SHAKESPEARE. VERY GOOD PLAYS. 'JULIUS CAESAR'! AND SHAW!

WHAT ABOUT ARAB WRITERS?

ALL FOOLS.

ANY GOOD ARAB LEADERS?

NO.

NOT NASSAR?

NO NO.

NO ONE?

SALADIN*

*SALADIN – 12th century Arab sultan who fought the crusades.

WE DON'T HAVE LEADERS. THE ARAB GOVERNMENTS ARE LIKE THE TAIL OF A SNAKE, AND THE HEAD OF THE SNAKE IS BRITAIN OR AMERICA. BUT THE WORST HAS BEEN BRITAIN.

HOW DO YOU THINK THE ISRAELIS WILL REACT, WILL THEY GET HARDER BECAUSE THREE OF THEIR SOLDIERS WERE KILLED?

HARDER SOFTER, SOFTER HARDER, IT DOESN'T MATTER... IT WILL GO ON FOREVER AND FOREVER.

WHAT ABOUT THE PEACE PROCESS?

IT WAS DEAD BEFORE IT WAS BORN. PEACE PROCESS, BEAST PROCESS.

J. SACCO

YOU DON'T THINK THE ISRAELIS WILL LEAVE?

THEY WILL NEVER LEAVE. THEY WILL ONLY FLEE.

YOU SEE THEM UP THERE, ON THE ROOFS, LOOKING? THEY MUST PAY ATTENTION...

ONCE THEY SLEEP WE WILL...

KKKKIK

CAN JEWS LIVE TOGETHER WITH PALESTINIANS IN SEPARATE STATES?

NEVER! THEY WANT THIS LAND, WE WANT THIS LAND. EVEN IF THEY GO BEHIND THE GREEN LINE, WHAT IF I OWN A CAVE BY HAIFA? THAT IS STILL MY CAVE!

SALAAM ALEEKUM.

ALEEKUM ES-SALAAM.

THIS MAN, HE HAD LAND AND A HOUSE ON THE OTHER SIDE OF THE GREEN LINE, THEY TOOK IT FROM HIM... THE ISRAELIS HAVE HIS OLIVE TREES NOW. ASK HIM IF HE WILL EVER GIVE UP THIS LAND...

WHAT'S HE SAYING?

HE SAYS IF THEY GAVE HIM ALL THE LAND BETWEEN HERE AND PAKISTAN, HE WOULDN'T GIVE UP A ROCK OF THE LAND THEY TOOK FROM HIM.

HAHAHA HAHA HAHA

YOU KNOW WHAT THIS PEACE PROCESS IS? IT IS OUR PALESTINIAN LEADERS SIGNING PAPERS TO MAKE WHAT THE ISRAELIS HAVE DONE LEGAL... BUT IT DOESN'T MATTER. LET THEM MAKE IT LEGAL...

IT DOESN'T CHANGE A THING!

J. SACCO 895

A BOY IN THE RAIN

I met an Irishman in Jerusalem, he was an Oxford student with plans for going into the Anglican priesthood, but his interests ranged over the entire Judeo-Christian spectrum... he was a connoisseur ...in fact, a real religions nut...

he did the Stations of the Cross with the Franciscans...

...joined the Armenian Orthodox for evening vespers...

...and you better believe he was rubbing his hands in the Church of the Holy Sepulchre...

Fridays, with a tefillin shelrosh strapped to his head, he was down at the Western Wall, lying outright about having a Jewish mother in order to get invited to Shabbat supper by the Hasidim...

Me, I didn't go for that jazz, I'd come to the same place but with a different theme — you know, the Palestinian question...

The Irishman, who could toss wonders with assorted olives and a few greens, was at the hostel for weeks, and we began sharing meals and our respective days' adventures...

he beamed about kissing the ring of the visiting Archbishop of Canterbury....

I held forth on Ramallah and its percussion grenades...

I suppose both our dreams were coming true...

J. SACCO 8 95

The one time our agendas intersected was in the West Bank town of Bethlehem, Christmas Eve...

He was there, of course, for Midnight Mass. Even I, a Catholic long lapsed, put in a genuflection at the Church of St. Catherine...

But it got old quick, with all the pilgrims pushing and shoving in dozens of languages, and, besides, a pillar blocked my view...

I left my Irish buddy, his eyes shut tight in concentration on the Latin, in search of my own particular brand of fodder among the on-edge Israeli soldiers and their security checks...

And I didn't need to look far — the mass was being shown (for those who hadn't elbowed their way into the church) on a big screen set up in Manger Square on the Israeli side of police head-quarters...

I dare say both the Irishman and I left Bethlehem that night thoroughly satisfied — he with another religious spectacle under his belt, I with one more of the occupation's mean ironies to gloat over...

but that's the thing about coming to the Holy Land or Palestine or Israel or whatever you want to call it...no one who knows what he's come here looking for leaves without having found it...

J. SACCO 8-95

280

And a few weeks later, on the bus out, bound for Cairo, I met a lady who had found what she'd come for, too...

She was Jewish, from New York, the large part of her family had been liquidated in the Holocaust, she'd been taken out of Germany in the nick of time... And she'd just spent three weeks of her vacation doing volunteer work for the Israeli army... She'd come to see the beautiful, vibrant, besieged Israel, and she wasn't leaving disappointed either...

ISRAEL IS WONDERFUL...

THE ISRAELIS ARE WONDERFUL...

IT'S SAD THOUGH, IT'S SAD, TO SEE THOSE YOUNG PEOPLE HAVING TO CARRY GUNS BECAUSE THERE'S ALWAYS A THREAT...

AND AFTER ALL THEIR PEOPLE HAVE BEEN THROUGH...

WELL, THERE'S ANOTHER SIDE TO THE STORY OF ISRAEL. THE PALESTINIANS—

ALL I'M SAYING IS I WANT PEACE.

Yes yes, we all want peace, whatever that is, but peace can mean different things, too, and isn't described identically by all who wish to imagine it...

One of my first days in Jerusalem, I found myself sitting in the back room of an Arab jewelry shop with a Palestinian, an Israeli, and two Americans who did press work for a non-governmental organization. We were analyzing the current peace process, envisioning, as one does, what, if anything, might work...

SOMETIMES I THINK ONE PLURALISTIC STATE OF ARABS AND JEWS WOULD MAKE THE MOST SENSE —IN THE LONG TERM, ANYWAY.

I THINK THE MOST PREVALENT IDEA IS THAT A TWO-STATE SOLUTION IS THE ONE WITH THE BEST CHANCE OF ACCEPTANCE AND SUCCESS.

J. SACCO 8-95

You could see the kids in the distance taking cover on each side of the road...

if we continued that way, we were going to get stoned...

The driver backed the bus up and turned it around...

he stopped at a small army post and asked for more directions...

ABOUT THE AUTHOR

photograph by Michael Tierney

Joe Sacco was born in Malta. He graduated from the University of Oregon with a degree in journalism. His first book, *Palestine*, won an American Book Award in 1996 and singlehandedly defined a new genre: graphic journalism. His work has since appeared in *Time*, *Harper's*, and *The Guardian*, amongst numerous other publications, and he was the recipient of a 2001 Guggenheim Fellowship. He lives in Portland, Oregon.

ALSO AVAILABLE FROM JOE SACCO & FANTAGRAPHICS BOOKS:

Safe Area Gorazde: The War in Eastern Bosnia, 1992-1995
Notes from a Defeatist
But I Like It
Palestine: The Special Editon
Safe Area Gorazde: The Special Edition
Bumf Vol. 1

OTHER BOOKS BY JOE SACCO:

The Fixer and Other Stories
Days of Destruction, Days of Revolt (with Chris Hedges)
Footnotes in Gaza
Journalism
The Great War: July 1, 1916